Intro to Economics:
Money, History, & Fiscal Faith

First printing: July 2017
Second printing: May 2019

Master Books®, P.O. Box 726, Green Forest, AR 72638

Master Books® is a division of the New Leaf Publishing Group, Inc.

ISBN: 978-1-68344-106-9
ISBN: 978-1-61458-626-5 (digital)

Unless otherwise noted, Scripture quotations are from the New King James Version of the Bible.

Printed in the United States of America

Please visit our website for other great titles:
www.masterbooks.com

For information regarding author interviews,
please contact the publicity department at (870) 438-5288.

"Your reputation as a publisher is stellar. It is a blessing knowing anything I purchase from you is going to be worth every penny!

—Cheri ★ ★ ★ ★ ★

"Last year we found Master Books and it has made a HUGE difference.

—Melanie ★ ★ ★ ★ ★

"We love Master Books and the way it's set up for easy planning!

—Melissa ★ ★ ★ ★ ★

"You have done a great job. MASTER BOOKS ROCKS!

—Stephanie ★ ★ ★ ★ ★

"Physically high-quality, Biblically faithful, and well-written.

—Danika ★ ★ ★ ★ ★

"Best books ever. Their illustrations are captivating and content amazing!

—Kathy ★ ★ ★ ★ ★

Affordable
Flexible
Faith Building

Table of Contents

Author Bios:

Jerry Robinson offers you the ultimate financial survival guide in *Bankruptcy of Our Nation*. Robinson, an economist, columnist, and radio host, is featured weekly on Worldnetdaily.com, quoted by *USA Today*, has appeared on Fox News, and has written columns for Townhall and FinancialSense.

Chad Hovind offers a way to take control of your financial future today! Use biblical wisdom to put yourself on a path of stability as you develop a deeper understanding of how the pursuit and management of money impacts your work and faith!

Features: The suggested weekly schedule enclosed has easy-to-manage lessons that guide the reading, worksheets, and all assessments. The pages of this guide are perforated and three-hole punched so materials are easy to tear out, hand out, grade, and store. Teachers are encouraged to adjust the schedule and materials needed in order to best work within their unique educational program.

Lesson Scheduling: Students are instructed to read the pages in their book and then complete the corresponding section provided by the teacher. Assessments that may include worksheets, activities, quizzes, and tests are given at regular intervals with space to record each grade. Space is provided on the weekly schedule for assignment dates, and flexibility in scheduling is encouraged. Teachers may adapt the scheduled days per each unique student situation. As the student completes each assignment, this can be marked with an "X" in the box.

🕐	Approximately 30 to 45 minutes per lesson, two days a week
🔑	Includes answer keys for worksheets, quizzes, semester, and final exams
✏️	Worksheets for each chapter
📄	Quizzes are included to help reinforce learning and provide assessment opportunities; optional semester and final exams included
🔁	Designed for grades 10 to 12 in a one-year course to earn ½ economics credit

Course Objectives: Students completing this course will

- Investigate the origins and history of various currencies
- Become familiar with biblical principles and insights with real-life examples for understanding God's views on money
- Identify the historical impact of the Federal Reserve, modern money mechanics, and other issues impacting the current money system in America
- Learn practical tips for avoiding debt, building your savings, spending wisely, and giving from a heart of grace
- Study simple guidelines for life and work God meant for us

Course Description

This is the suggested course sequence that allows one core area of economics to be studied per semester. You can change the sequence of the semesters per the needs or interests of your student; materials for each semester are independent of one another to allow flexibility. Students may want to have a notebook or blank paper handy for questions that require more lengthy responses.

Bankruptcy of Our Nation

The message of this course is one of great hope. Our hope is in knowing which direction the trends are taking us, and to sense God's leading through every step. It is in this knowledge that you will be able to understand the basics of economics and how to make good financial decisions. Despite man's best efforts, God is still in control, and with God, the end is only the beginning. Be prepared to examine in-depth how the purchasing power of our U.S. dollar is declining in value, why the U.S. government continues to print more money, what keeps us endlessly engaged in an expensive and endless global war on terror, why our national debt is at an all-time high and growing exponentially, and ultimately how to break free from the consumption trap in *Bankruptcy of Our Nation*.

Money Wise DVD

Money Wise is a fun, engaging, and fact-filled DVD journey into God's wisdom on work and money.

Throughout *Money Wise*, Chad Hovind explores God's principles, His teachings, and His directions for living a life of liberty, prosperity, and generosity. Chad presents a biblical case for free-market enterprise, and offers God's perspective for the economic decisions of an individual, a family, and even a nation.

Money Wise explains that God wants us to live a life of freedom to serve Him, to provide for ourselves, and to bless others.

Special Note to Parents:

Bankruptcy of Our Nation is written at a high-school age level and beyond. Please be aware of three minor instances in the book that you may want to review before allowing your student, depending on their age and maturity level, to read it. They are:

Page 94: a quote on the page uses a word that some may find offensive

Page 148: this page uses a comparative reference to suicide by firearm

Page 194: in a discussion on American addictions, the word "sex" is used

While these instances do not directly impact the context and focus of this curriculum, we feel it is important that parents be made aware of any item that may or may not impact their learner so the parent can make decisions and take action they feel is necessary in that instance. By making parents aware, we seek to ensure parents and students are not blindsided by these few references.

First Semester Suggested Daily Schedule

Date	Day	Assignment	Due Date	✓	Grade
		First Semester-First Quarter			
	Day 1				
	Day 2	What Would God Say to Adam Smith? **Economics Worksheet 1** • Pages 15–16 • Teacher Guide • (TG) Watch Session 1: Adam Smith • *Money Wise* DVD • (MW)	*September 16*		
Week 1	Day 3				
	Day 4	Session 1: Adam Smith • **Economics Worksheet 2** • Pages 17–20 • (TG)			
	Day 5				
	Day 6				
	Day 7	What Would God Say to John Keynes? **Economics Worksheet 1** • Pages 21–22 • (TG) Watch Session 2: John Keynes • (MW)	*Sept 17th*		
Week 2	Day 8				
	Day 9	Session 2: John Keynes • **Economics Worksheet 2** • Pages 23–26 • (TG)			
	Day 10				
	Day 11				
	Day 12	What Would God Say to F.D.R? **Economics Worksheet 1** • Pages 27–28 • (TG) Watch Session 3: F.D.R. • (MW)	*Sept 18*		
Week 3	Day 13				
	Day 14	Session 3: F.D.R. • **Economics Worksheet 2** • Pages 29–32 • (TG)			
	Day 15				
	Day 16				
	Day 17	What Would God Say to Alan Greenspan? **Economics Worksheet 1** • Pages 33–34 • (TG) Watch Session 4: Alan Greenspan • (MW)	*Sept 19*		
Week 4	Day 18				
	Day 19	Session 4: Greenspan • **Economics Worksheet 2** • Pages 35–38 • (TG)			
	Day 20				
	Day 21				
	Day 22	What Would God Say to Karl Marx? **Economics Worksheet 1** • Pages 39–40 • (TG) Watch Session 5: Karl Marx • (MW)	*Sept 20*		
Week 5	Day 23				
	Day 24	Session 5: Karl Marx • **Economics Worksheet 2** • Page 41 • (TG)			
	Day 25				
	Day 26				
	Day 27	Session 5: Karl Marx • **Economics Worksheet 3** • Pages 43–44 • (TG)			
Week 6	Day 28				
	Day 29	Session 5: Karl Marx • **Economics Worksheet 4** • Pages 45–48 • (TG)			
	Day 30				

Date	Day	Assignment	Due Date	✓	Grade
Week 7	Day 31				
	Day 32	What Would God Say to the I.R.S.? **Economics Worksheet 1** • Pages 49–50 • (TG) Watch Session 6: The I.R.S. • (MW)			
	Day 33				
	Day 34	Session 6: The I.R.S. • **Economics Worksheet 2** • Pages 51–54 • (TG)			
	Day 35				
Week 8	Day 36				
	Day 37	**Money Wise Sessions 1-6** • **Quiz 1** • Pages 187–188 • (TG)			
	Day 38				
	Day 39	**Project Economics Worksheet 1** • Pages 55–56 • (TG)			
	Day 40				
Week 9	Day 41				
	Day 42	Whistle While You Work **Economics Worksheet 1** • Page 57 • (TG) Watch Session 7: Work • (MW)			
	Day 43				
	Day 44	Session 7: Work • **Economics Worksheet 2** • Pages 59–62 • (TG)			
	Day 45				

First Semester-Second Quarter

Date	Day	Assignment	Due Date	✓	Grade
Week 1	Day 46				
	Day 47	Whistle While You Profit **Economics Worksheet 1** • Pages 63–64 • (TG) Watch Session 8: Profit • (MW)			
	Day 48				
	Day 49	Session 8: Profit • **Economics Worksheet 2** • Pages 65–70 • (TG)			
	Day 50				
Week 2	Day 51				
	Day 52	Whistle While You Lead **Economics Worksheet 1** • Pages 71–72 • (TG) Watch Session 9: Lead • (MW)			
	Day 53				
	Day 54	Session 9: Lead • **Economics Worksheet 2** • Pages 73–76 • (TG)			
	Day 55				
Week 3	Day 56				
	Day 57	Whistle While You Rest **Economics Worksheet 1** • Page 77 • (TG) Watch Session 10: Rest • (MW)			
	Day 58				
	Day 59	Session 10: Rest • **Economics Worksheet 2** • Pages 79–82 • (TG)			
	Day 60				

Date	Day	Assignment	Due Date	✓	Grade
Week 4	Day 61				
	Day 62	Session 10: Rest • **Economics Worksheet 3** • Pages 83–86 • (TG)			
	Day 63				
	Day 64	Session 10: Rest • **Economics Worksheet 4** • Pages 87–88 • (TG)			
	Day 65				
Week 5	Day 66				
	Day 67	Whistle While You Give **Economics Worksheet 1** • Page 89 • (TG) Watch Session 11: Give • (MW)			
	Day 68				
	Day 69	Session 11: Give • **Economics Worksheet 2** • Pages 91–96 • (TG)			
	Day 70				
Week 6	Day 71				
	Day 72	Whistle While You Manage **Economics Worksheet 1** • Page 97 • (TG) Watch Session 12: Manage • (MW)			
	Day 73				
	Day 74	Session 12: Manage • **Economics Worksheet 2** • Pages 99–104 • (TG)			
	Day 75				
Week 7	Day 76				
	Day 77	Whistle While You Spend **Economics Worksheet 1** • Pages 105–106 • (TG) Watch Session 13: Spend • (MW)			
	Day 78				
	Day 79	Session 13: Spend • **Economics Worksheet 2** • Pages 107–112 • (TG)			
	Day 80				
Week 8	Day 81				
	Day 82	Boaz: Whistle While You Serve **Economics Worksheet 1** • Page 113 • (TG) Watch Session 14: Boaz • (MW)			
	Day 83				
	Day 84	**Common Sense Economics Sessions 7–14** **Quiz 2** • Pages 189–190 • (TG)			
	Day 85				
Week 9	Day 86				
	Day 87	**Economics Sessions 1-14 • Test** • Page 197–198 • (TG)			
	Day 88				
	Day 89	**Project Economics Worksheet 2** • Pages 115 • (TG)			
	Day 90				
		Mid-Term Grade			

Second Semester Suggested Daily Schedule

Date	Day	Assignment	Due Date	✓	Grade
		Second Semester-Third Quarter			
Week 1	Day 91				
	Day 92	Introduction • Read Pages 7–15 • *Bankruptcy of Our Nation* • (BN) • **Economics Worksheet 1** • Page 119 • Teacher Guide • (TG)			
	Day 93				
	Day 94	Introduction • **Economics Worksheet 2** • Page 121 • (TG)			
	Day 95				
Week 2	Day 96				
	Day 97	Ch 1: What Is Money...Really? Read Pages 17–30 • (BN) • **Economics Worksheet 1** • Page 123 • (TG)			
	Day 98				
	Day 99	Ch 1: What Is Money...Really? **Economics Worksheet 2** • Pages 125–126 • (TG)			
	Day 100				
Week 3	Day 101				
	Day 102	Ch 2: A Short History of Fiat Currencies Read Pages 31–50 • (BN)			
	Day 103				
	Day 104	Ch 2: A Short History of Fiat Currencies **Economics Worksheet 1** • Page 127 • (TG)			
	Day 105				
Week 4	Day 106				
	Day 107	Ch 2: A Short History of Fiat Currencies **Economics Worksheet 2** • Pages 129–130 • (TG)			
	Day 108				
	Day 109	Ch 2: A Short History of Fiat Currencies **Economics Worksheet 3** • Pages 131–132 • (TG)			
	Day 110				
Week 5	Day 111				
	Day 112	Ch 3: The Rise and Fall of the Golden Permission Slip Read Pages 51-63 • (BN) • **Economics Worksheet 1** • Page 133 • (TG)			
	Day 113				
	Day 114	Ch 3: The Rise and Fall of the Golden Permission Slip **Economics Worksheet 2** • Pages 135–136 • (TG)			
	Day 115				
Week 6	Day 116				
	Day 117	Ch 4: The Petrodollar System Read Pages 65–78 • (BN) • **Economics Worksheet 1** • Page 137 • (TG)			
	Day 118				
	Day 119	Ch 4: The Petrodollar System **Economics Worksheet 2** • Pages 139–140 • (TG)			
	Day 120				

Date	Day	Assignment	Due Date	✓	Grade
Week 7	Day 121				
	Day 122	Ch 5: Petrodollar Wars Read Pages 79–96 • (BN) • **Economics Worksheet 1** • Page 141 • (TG)			
	Day 123				
	Day 124	Ch 5: Petrodollar Wars • **Economics Worksheet 2** • Pages 143-144 • (TG)			
	Day 125				
Week 8	Day 126				
	Day 127	Ch 6: The History of the Federal Reserve • Read Pages 97–118 • (BN)			
	Day 128				
	Day 129	Ch 6: The History of the Federal Reserve **Economics Worksheet 1** • Page 145 • (TG)			
	Day 130				
Week 9	Day 131				
	Day 132	Ch 6: The History of the Federal Reserve **Economics Worksheet 2** • Pages 147–148 • (TG)			
	Day 133				
	Day 134	Ch 6: The History of the Federal Reserve **Economics Worksheet 3** • Pages 149–152 • (TG)			
	Day 135				
		Second Semester-Fourth Quarter			
Week 1	Day 136				
	Day 137	Ch 6: The History of the Federal Reserve **Economics Worksheet 4** • Pages 153–156 • (TG)			
	Day 138				
	Day 139	**Bankruptcy of Our Nation Chapters 1–6 • Quiz 1** • Pages 191–194 • (TG)			
	Day 140				
Week 2	Day 141				
	Day 142	Ch 7: Modern Money Mechanics Read Pages 119–136 • (BN) • **Economics Worksheet 1** • Page 157 • (TG)			
	Day 143				
	Day 144	Ch 7: Modern Money Mechanics **Economics Worksheet 2** • Pages 159–160 • (TG)			
	Day 145				
Week 3	Day 146				
	Day 147	Ch 7: Modern Money Mechanics **Economics Worksheet 3** • Pages 161–162 • (TG)			
	Day 148				
	Day 149	Ch 8: America: The Greatest Debtor Nation in World History Read Pages 137–153 • (BN) • **Economics Worksheet 1** • Page 163 • (TG)			
	Day 150				

Date	Day	Assignment	Due Date	✓	Grade
Week 4	Day 151				
	Day 152	Ch 8: America: The Greatest Debtor Nation in World History **Economics Worksheet 2** • Pages 165–166 • (TG)			
	Day 153				
	Day 154	Ch 9: The Retirement Crisis Read Pages 155–165 • (BN) • **Economics Worksheet 1** • Page 167 • (TG)			
	Day 155				
Week 5	Day 156				
	Day 157	Ch 9: The Retirement Crisis **Economics Worksheet 2** • Pages 169–170 • (TG)			
	Day 158				
	Day 159	Ch 10: The Coming American Hyperinflation and Dollar Collapse Read Pages 167–190 • (BN) • **Economics Worksheet 1** • Page 171 • (TG)			
	Day 160				
Week 6	Day 161				
	Day 162	Ch 10: The Coming American Hyperinflation and Dollar Collapse **Economics Worksheet 2** • Pages 173–176 • (TG)			
	Day 163				
	Day 164	Ch 11: Maxed Out: The New American Slavery Read Pages 191–203 • (BN) • **Economics Worksheet 1** • Page 177 • (TG)			
	Day 165				
Week 7	Day 166				
	Day 167	Ch 11: Maxed Out: The New American Slavery **Economics Worksheet 2** • Pages 179–180 • (TG)			
	Day 168				
	Day 169	Ch 12: Breaking Free from the Consumption Trap • Read Pages 205–216 • (BN) • **Economics Worksheet 1** • Page 181 • (TG)			
	Day 170				
Week 8	Day 171				
	Day 172	Ch 12: Breaking Free from the Consumption Trap **Economics Worksheet 2** • Pages 183–184 • (TG)			
	Day 173				
	Day 174	**Bankruptcy of Our Nation: Chs 7–12 Quiz 2** • Pages 195–196 • (TG)			
	Day 175				
Week 9	Day 176				
	Day 177	**Bankruptcy of Our Nation: Chs 1–12 Test** • Pages 199–200 • (TG)			
	Day 178				
	Day 179	**Economics Final Test** • Pages 201–202 • (TG)			
	Day 180				
		Final Grade			

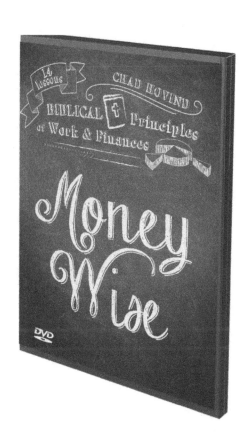

Economic Worksheets

for Use with

Money Wise **DVDs**

Soak in the Sure Sayings

"The natural effort of every individual to better his own condition . . . is so powerful a principle, that it is alone capable of carrying on the society to wealth and prosperity . . . surmounting a hundred obstructions with which the folly of human laws too often encumbers its operations. The drive for greater government regulation is the drive toward increased poverty, unemployment, and the loss of liberty."

—Adam Smith*

Introduction

In this first session of *Godonomics*, you will learn the basics of capitalism, profit, and work. You'll discover that the father of modern capitalism was a Christian named Adam Smith who showed how God's principles of liberty, prosperity, and generosity could change an individual, a family, and even a national economy — and it sure did! As his principles were applied, a wave of prosperity washed across Europe and spilled into America in the 1800s. We'll see that profit truly is a gift from God when it is focused on meeting others' needs rather than personal greed.

Many employers today are finding that many lack the proper business skills to launch from college into the work force. Session 1 covers some basics of running a business and how to pay employees and set up pay scales in your company in a way that pays people fairly, not equally.

In addition, this session gives us an example of how to teach our kids a strong work ethic and eliminate the entitlement attitude that keeps our kids and our society from experiencing their full potential. If you've ever felt the strain of a family member who is mooching off you, this chapter helps you understand that there are times to help those in need and times not to enable others' bad behavior.

Matthew 25:26–28

But his lord answered and said to him, "You wicked and lazy servant, you knew that I reap where I have not sown, and gather where I have not scattered seed. So you ought to have deposited my money with the bankers, and at my coming I would have received back my own with interest. Therefore take the talent from him, and give it to him who has ten talents."

Proverbs 31 sums up how a good economy works: The Proverbs 31 woman begins by finding a vineyard that produces. She profits from it. Then from her savings, she invests in another vineyard, allowing her to give to the poor and needy, hire more workers, and spend. This Bible passage demonstrates the power of the free market — affirming property rights, incentive, and freedom.

$hare in Prayer

$ee the Godly Perspective

Is profit a good thing or a bad thing? Since God offered his wisdom on so many subjects, doesn't it make sense that He'd offer wisdom on principles of economics, too? Let's look at our own finances from God's perspective. Is God in control of them? On a national scale, in the time it will have taken you to read this sentence, the United States national debt will have increased by about $200,000. Surely, runaway debt is not a result of godly principles. How different would things be if we instituted *Godonomics* at every level of society?

* *The Wealth Of Nations*, Book IV, Chapter V, Digression on the Corn Trade, p. 540, para. b 43.; www.adamsmith.org/; "What Would God Say to Adam Smith?", *Godonomics* DVD.

$earch For Truth

In this first session, notice the failure of socialism's early experiment in America's history. Note how a centralized approach to economics is both inefficient and unscriptural. Learn what source Adam Smith turned to for direction when socialism failed.

Throughout history, Christ's followers have succeeded in many areas where others have failed, including financial endeavors, simply by following God's Word. Watch for God's foundational sequence laid out in this first session of Production, Profit, and Savings. This approach to capitalism stands in stark contrast to the consumer-based approach commonly accepted today. *Godonomics* is all about following God's order in finances, which leads to greater ability and freedom to serve God, to provide for ourselves, and to bless others. A reoccurring theme throughout our study will be that God desperately wants us to experience liberty, prosperity, and generosity. Let's delve into the first principles of *GODONOMICS* — the Gift of Work, and the Gift of Profit!

2 Thessalonians 3:7–9

For you yourselves know how you ought to follow us, for we were not disorderly among you; nor did we eat anyone's bread free of charge, but worked with labor and toil night and day, that we might not be a burden to any of you, not because we do not have authority, but to make ourselves an example of how you should follow us.

$tart the DVD $ession 1

(32 minutes)

1. When he landed in America, Governor _____ tried an experiment in socialism that ended in disaster.

Three components of capitalism are:

2. _____

3. _____ (or liberty)

4. and _____.

In 1776, Adam Smith, the Father of Modern Capitalism, wrote a book entitled
5. _____, which included godly principles of capitalism that eventually influenced the structure of the U.S. economy.

God wants us to experience

6. _____

7. _____

8. _____

9. The Gift of _____.
   • Work is from God: Genesis 2:15
   • Work for God: Colossians 3:23–24
   • Work for self-sufficiency to bear your own load: Galatians 6:4–5
   • Work is mandated in 2 Thessalonians 3:7–12, affirming the components of capitalism.

10. The Gift of _____.

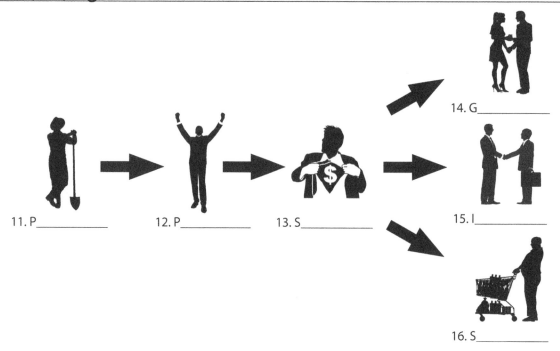

11. P_____
12. P_____
13. S_____
14. G_____
15. I_____
16. S_____

Proverbs 31

She considers a field and buys it; from her profits she plants a vineyard. . . . She perceives that her merchandise is good, and her lamp does not go out by night. . . . She extends her hand to the poor, yes, she reaches out her hands to the needy. . . . And does not eat the bread of idleness. . . . Give her of the fruit of her hands. . . .

Treat and pay people 17. _____, not 18. _____.

"The drive for greater government regulation is a drive toward increased

19. _____, 20. _____, and the loss of

21. _____."

God the father loved us so much, that He sent His son, Jesus Christ, to earth to die for us. As a believer in Jesus Christ, we are 22. _____ 23. _____ with Him to all the riches of a loving Heavenly Father!

(Romans 8:17: "And if children, then heirs — heirs of God, and joint-heirs with Christ. . . .")

$ettle the Discussion Questions

1. What are three primary elements of *Godonomics*-style capitalism, and how might each of them facilitate a more prosperous and Christian lifestyle?

2. Socialism seeks to control and intervene in the economy to treat people equally, but how might laissez-faire — free market capitalism — be a better system, and in what way might a government-run economy be contrary to Scripture?

3. What is *Godonomics*? What are the steps an individual should follow concerning their finances according to this model?

$tudy the $ummary $tatements

When we follow God's rules and model for economics, we will work as unto the Lord, yielding a profit. In turn, we will be able to give and to invest. In Proverbs 13:22, the Bible tells us, "A good man leaves an inheritance to his children's children." In reality, this is no magic potion. *Godonomics* is not a get-rich-quick scheme. It is a set of godly principles in which one is not enslaved to debt. Income is real profit, something more than just a means to make the monthly payments. When *Godonomics* is applied on a national scale, the national economy, too, is as prosperous as the laborers and investors are willing to labor to produce. Protecting property rights and seeking limited government allows the incentives of honest profits to reward those who take the initiative.

2 Thessalonians 3:10–12

For even when we were with you, we commanded you this: If anyone will not work, neither shall he eat. For we hear that there are some who walk among you in a disorderly manner, not working at all, but are busybodies. Now those who are such we command and exhort through our Lord Jesus Christ that they work in quietness and eat their own bread.

Instilling these principles of investing, saving, and working in our children is also important. We need to train our children to seek fair reward for their labors — not equal benefits.

Throughout history, God has blessed individuals and nations who worked hard for their profit and honored Him with their increase. We can be assured that everyone has their own work interest at heart. However, when yielded to God, our labor can lead to prosperity and greater generosity, promoting both self-sufficiency and the ability to give and meet the needs of society as the Lord leads. These principles form the bedrock of *Godonomics*.

$how $upport

Read each of the following sentences and the verses that go with them. After you've read all eight, discuss the following questions.

As a whole, how would society be better if we followed God's principles of work?

Which of the employee/employer commandments stand out to you?

What the Bible says to an employer:

1. Serve, not "use," my employees by paying them fairly (Matthew 20:26).

2. Hold my employees accountable (Matthew 16:27).

3. Pay my employees fairly and promptly (Malachi 3:5; Deuteronomy 24:14–15).

4. Work like God is your boss (Colossians 3:23–24).

What the Bible says to an employee:

1. Work hard and diligently (Ecclesiastes 9:10).

2. Work honestly by not cheating your boss (Daniel 6:4).

3. Don't be lazy (2 Thessalonians 3:10).

4. Work like God is your boss (Colossians 3:23–24).

$cripture to $avor

2 Thessalonians 3:8–10

. . . nor did we eat anyone's bread free of charge, but worked with labor and toil night and day, that we might not be a burden to any of you, not because we do not have authority, but to make ourselves an example of how you should follow us. For even when we were with you, we commanded you this: If anyone will not work, neither shall he eat.

"So . . . What Would God Say to Adam Smith?"

Who's your barber?

Work, property rights, and incentives are blessings from Me.

— God

Soak in the Sure Sayings

"A government big enough to give you everything you want, is big enough to take away everything you have."

—Gerald R. Ford*

Introduction

In our second session, "What Would God Say to John Keynes?" we'll discover how Keynesian economics and *Godonomics* are polar opposites! Even if you have never heard of John Keynes, you witness daily how his ideas are today's blueprint for the concept of money management as well as the economic policies of most governments. Individuals, marriages, and nations are all under severe stress from debt caused by spending more than we have and paying ever-increasing interest on credit. Our children are losing their liberty as our national debt skyrockets into the trillions of dollars. Proverbs tells us to leave an inheritance to our children's children, not a bill from our gluttonous spending.

Delve into Session Two of *Godonomics* where we'll learn two important slogans: "Spend your way to slavery, not prosperity!" and "Act your own wage!"

Matthew 25:24–29

Then he who had received the one talent came and said, "Lord, I knew you to be a hard man, reaping where you have not sown, and gathering where you have not scattered seed. And I was afraid, and went and hid your talent in the ground. Look, there you have what is yours." But his lord answered and said to him, "You wicked and lazy servant, you knew that I reap where I have not sown, and gather where I have not scattered seed. So you ought to have deposited my money with the bankers, and at my coming I would have received back my own with interest. Therefore take the talent from him, and give it to him who has ten talents. For to everyone who has, more will be given, and he will have abundance; but from him who does not have, even what he has will be taken away."

$hare in Prayer

$ee the Godly Perspective

John Keynes thought he had a new idea: borrow your way out of debt. He taught that governments could step in and solve national economic problems by offsetting demand — thus requiring excessive debt, inflation, and loss of personal liberty. Throughout this session, notice that God addressed this idea long ago and made it quite clear that debt produces slavery, not freedom or success.

$earch for Truth

In recent years, the U.S. government has "bailed out" failing businesses, claiming that they were just too big to let them fail. It may have sounded charitable to give money to companies that had poorly managed their assets and budgets with the intention of saving jobs, but where did that money come from? Governments do not have money of their own. Government must obtain money from: 1) taxing producers, 2) inflating the currency, or 3) borrowing from other nations. A "bailout" is not producing a solution. It is merely

* (Widely attributed to Thomas Jefferson, though it does not appear in any known writings of his. www.Fordlibrarymuseum.gov/grf/quotes.asp)

rearranging and increasing debt, which is not only harmful, but unscriptural. In all three of these options, one group is helped while another is severely hurt, whether it be from increasing prices for everyone because of inflation, higher taxes for future generations from borrowing, or lost jobs caused by downsizing when producers are forced to deal with increased taxation.

In this episode we'll see that the intent of Keynesian economics was not to glorify God, but to glorify man and destroy biblical economics. Watch as the two worldviews stand in stark contrast: one supporting greed by giving man whatever he wants whenever he wants it, and the other supporting contentment by providing for the needy, working hard, and glorifying God through honest labor and profit.

Watch as followers of John Keynes seek to dig their way out of the hole of debt by borrowing, taxing producers, and inflating currency (printing more money out of thin air). All three actually damage the economy. Notice that, contrary to this worldly system, God gave us a better plan. *Godonomics* allows us to use material things like money to help our fellow man and ourselves. Observe throughout this session that according to the Bible, debt is not the solution — it is the problem!

$tart the DVD $ession

(33 minutes)

Both sides of the U.S. political structure follow the economic ideas of

1. _____ 2. _____.

3. John Keynes' wisdom on money is almost the direct _____ of what God teaches about money.

4. John Keynes ultimately moves you toward a _____ minset.

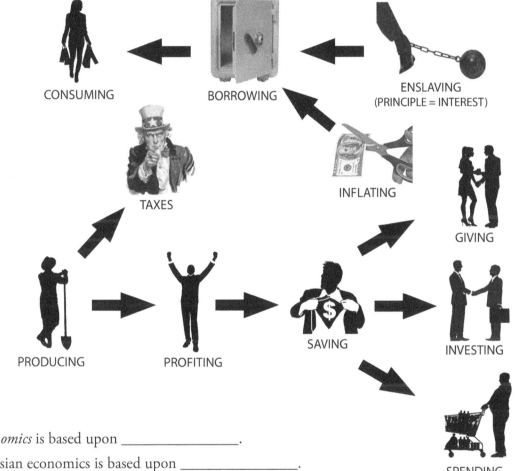

CONSUMING · BORROWING · ENSLAVING (PRINCIPLE = INTEREST) · TAXES · INFLATING · GIVING · PRODUCING · PROFITING · SAVING · INVESTING · SPENDING

5. *Godonomics* is based upon _____.

6. Keynesian economics is based upon _____.

US National Debt:

You can divide the US national debt by the number of American citizens to see each person's "share" of this debt.* Dividing it by taxpayers increases the amount per person. For example:

$17,559,060,160,057.74 (as of March 18, 2014)

Divided by 317,297,938 US citizens (as of January 1, 2014)=$55,339.35 per citizen

Divided by 146,243,886 taxpayers (individual returns in 2013)=$120,066.97 per taxpayer

You can also research historical data on daily amounts of the national debt at a US Department of the Treasury and Bureau of the Public Debt website.**

7. John Keynes wanted to destroy _____.

* www.usdebtclock.org; **www.treasurydirect.gov/NP/debt/current

8. Remember: *Godonomics* is about God wanting us to experience three components: liberty, prosperity, and _____.

Godonomics Slogan #1:

We Spend Our Way to Slavery, Not Prosperity!

9. Borrowing leads to _____.

If you owe your bank manager a thousand pounds, you are at his mercy. If you owe him a million pounds, he is at your mercy. — John Keynes

Romans 13:8

Owe no one anything except to love one another, for he who loves another has fulfilled the law.

Proverbs 22:7

The borrower is servant to the lender.

10. The principles of *Godonomics* applies to _____ as well as families and individuals.

11. God wants us _____.

Godonomics Slogan #2:

Act Your Own Wage!

In order to act our own wage, Christians must look:

12. _____ Luke 12:34 — Where your treasure is, there your heart will be also.

13. _____ Proverbs 13:7 — There are some who pretend to be rich, yet have nothing. There are some who pretend to be poor, yet have great wealth (World English Bible).

14. _____ Matthew 25:15–16, 20 — And to one he gave five talents, to another two, and to another one, to each according to his own ability; and immediately he went on a journey. Then he who had received the five talents went and traded with them, and made another five talents. . . . So he who had received five talents came and brought five other talents, saying, "Lord, you delivered to me five talents; look, I have gained five more talents besides them."

"Reason does not suffer us to admit that all usury is to be condemned without exception . . . that is only as to the poor. If we have to do with the rich, that usury is freely permitted. . . . Usury is not now unlawful. Let each one, then, place himself before God's judgment-seat, and not do to his neighbor what he would not have done to himself." — John Calvin*

15. The material world is not bad; money can be used for _____.

* Commentaries on the *Four Last Books of Moses*, arranged in the form of harmony, by John Calvin, Vol. 3, pp.131-132, Edinburgh: Printed for the Calvin Translation Society, December 1855.

I Timothy 6:10

For the love of money is the root of all evil: which while some coveted after, they have erred from the faith, and pierced themselves through with many sorrows (KJV).

The reformer 16. _____ 17. _____ produced a new way of thinking regarding money and interest; thus producing a wave of prosperity.

18. Jesus comes to offer us something money can't buy: _____.

We owe God a spiritual debt we cannot 19. _____, so Jesus 20. _____ it for us.

1 John 2:2

And He Himself is the propitiation for our sins, and not for ours only, but also for the whole world.

Deuteronomy 28:12, 43–44

The LORD will open to you His good treasure. . . . You shall lend to many nations, but you shall not borrow. . . . The alien who is among you shall rise higher and higher above you, and you shall come down lower and lower. He shall lend to you, but you shall not lend to him; he shall be the head, and you shall be the tail.

$ettle the Discussion Questions

1. Historically, Democrats tax and spend, Republicans borrow and spend, and both parties inflate and spend. How might the biblical principles of free enterprise, budgeting, and limited spending provide a solution to budget deficits and a lagging economy?

2. Keynes said, "If you owe your bank manager a thousand pounds, you are at his mercy. If you owe him a million pounds, he is at your mercy." If a person believes this quote by Keynes, how might that person address his own debt?

3. How is the focus of *Godonomics* different from that of Keynesian economics?

$tudy the $ummary $tatements

In America, both sides of the political establishment are Keynesians, and so the "debate" often excludes actual solutions. The options discussed are only matters of how much regulation or debt is necessary, which way we should spend more than we have, and how we can build government revenue via taxation, borrowing, or inflation. *Godonomics* teaches us to stop spending and to stop borrowing.

Both governments and individuals should stop living outside of their means. The solution to our debt problems is not to get another credit card, but to stop the spending. This is true at any level of the economy. Keynesian wisdom promotes our needs and wants as a top priority, even if we can't afford them. This yields an "entitlement mentality" of believing we deserve what we can't afford. However, God tells us to be content with the things we have — and only God can offer true and lasting contentment. Rather than practicing Keynesian economics and being enslaved to debt and our own selfish desires, we have the opportunity to practice *Godonomics* and experience true economic and spiritual freedom through Jesus Christ.

$how $upport

1 Timothy 6:6

"Now godliness with contentment is great gain."

List at least one way you want to see our nation practice *Godonomics* contentment rather than Keynesian economics greed in our national economy.

List at least one way you want to practice *Godonomics* contentment rather than Keynesian economics greed in your personal life.

$cripture to $avor

Proverbs 22:7

The rich rules over the poor, and the borrower is servant to the lender.

So . . . What Would God Say to John Keynes?

Stop overspending and stop borrowing!
— God

Soak in the Sure Sayings

"How do we find freedom? It is simple enough. We do not follow the path to poverty, consuming more than we produce. Instead we follow the path to prosperity, producing more than we consume. Don't sell tomorrow's labor for today's consumption!"

— R.C. Sproul Jr.*

In this third session of *Godonomics*, "What Would God Say to F.D.R.?" we'll discuss two more paramount principles from *Godonomics*: Number One — "Don't exchange borrowing for budgeting!" and Number Two — "Don't exchange liberty for security!" In our exposure and education about the Great Depression, most of us were taught that Franklin Delano Roosevelt's "New Deal" rescued our national economy. By taking a closer look at F.D.R.'s economic politics through the eyeglass of *Godonomic* principles, we'll discover that the Great Depression was worsened by his overspending, overinflating, and overborrowing. As we continue to use F.D.R.'s template in the current economic crisis, the results will be the same unless we understand and apply another *Godonomic* principle for dealing with a financial crisis — simply spend less than we make. Responsible spending must be practiced by ourselves. We, in turn, must teach our children these truths, for *Godonomics* can revolutionize our national economics!

James 4:13–14

Come now, you who say, "Today or tomorrow we will go to such and such a city, spend a year there, buy and sell, and make a profit"; whereas you do not know what will happen tomorrow. For what is your life? It is even a vapor that appears for a little time and then vanishes away.

$hare in Prayer

$ee the Godly Perspective

When we buy things on credit, we are spending tomorrow's money today. Would God be pleased with this lack of responsibility? Ephesians teaches that we should redeem the time because the days are evil, and Proverbs instructs us that we should leave an inheritance for our children's children. Debt robs us of this opportunity. When we buy things today with money we don't have, we are pushing back the consequences of our actions until another day. God's way, however, is to produce in order to spend, not to borrow in order to spend.

$earch for Truth

Keep an eye out for what God would say to F.D.R. throughout this episode: Don't spend tomorrow's money today. It's that simple. Greed often tricks our minds into believing we must have something — even at the expense of increasing debt. Notice that this seems to be the ongoing problem with both sides of the political aisle in America, and that a third way — God's way — needs to be followed.

Chad says in this session: "It's unwise to spend all of today's money today. It's foolish to spend all of tomorrow's money today, but it's immoral to spend someone else's money today." Listen carefully to the admonition of Proverbs 15:22 regarding inheritance and reflect on the stark contrast to what was passed down to future generations by F.D.R.

* *Biblical Economics*, R. C. Sproul, Jr. Tolle Lege Press: Powder Springs, GA; 2009

Finally, listen for the only path to true and lasting prosperity. Looking to the government as our security and solution leaves us unable to experience the true liberty and security God has for His followers!

$tart the DVD $ession

(33 minutes)

Both sides of the American political structure practice two unscriptural things:

1. _____ and 2. _____ .

Exchange #1:

Don't Exchange 3. _____ for 4. _____.

Don't Spend 5. _____ money 6. _____!

Proverbs 21:20

There is desirable treasure, and oil in the dwelling of the wise, but a foolish man squanders it.

The 7. _____ man 8. _____ all of today's money today and sometimes even consumes some of tomorrow's money today!

The 9. _____ man 10. _____ some of today's profits so he can invest in tomorrow's ventures, jobs, and expansions.

Applying this principle of *Godonomics* allows the wise man to:

• Be radically generous

• Invest in future economic endeavors with available capital

• Spend wisely

Proverbs 15:22

Without counsel, plans go awry, but in the multitude of counselors they are established.

11. A good man leaves an _____ to his children's children.

Borrowing money from the future is "12. _____ 13. _____."

We don't break 14. _____ 15. _____, we discover them.

16. What caused the Great Depression? Deficit _____

17. What brought us out of the Great Depression? _____

An infusion of borrowed money into an economy — personal or national — can appear to be prosperity at first, when in fact, it is only a "sugar high" that will eventually crash.

Luke 12:15

And He said to them, "Take heed and beware of covetousness, for one's life does not consist in the abundance of the things he possesses."

18. Budgeting is actually writing down your economic _____.

Ecclesiastes 11:2

Give a serving to seven, and also to eight, for you do not know what evil will be on the earth.

19. This passage teaches that because we live in an evil world, we should prepare for difficult times by _____ our savings.

20. Don't _____ upon unknown income and economic gain.

Exchange #2:

Don't exchange 21. _____ for 22. _____.

23. Governments have no _____.

First Samuel 8:4–9 warns that whatever a king offers in 24. _____, he will take away from your 25. _____.

26. First Samuel 8:19 says, "Nevertheless the people _____ the voice of Samuel; and they said, No; but we will have a king over us."

27. When Israel chose a king, the king _____ them, hurting their ability to produce, profit, save, and give.

Throughout history, Christ followers have wanted 28. _____ 29. _____.

30. Surrendering to King _____ and His wisdom yields true security and liberty.

Habakkuk 2:2

". . . Write the vision; and make it plain on tablets, that he may run who reads it."

Ephesians 5:16

". . . redeeming the time, because the days are evil."

Galatians 5:13

For you, brethren, have been called to liberty; only do not use liberty as an opportunity for the flesh, but through love serve one another.

For further study: If you are interested in more information about Hoover's deficit spending, and the depression within the depression caused by the policies of FDR, go to www.cato.org. The Cato Institute is a libertarian think tank of scholars that have done mountains of research on the Great Depression, how FDR's policies prolonged the Great Depression, and how free market policies actually solved the Great Depression of 1920.

"I am in favor of cutting taxes under any circumstances and for any excuse, for any reason, whenever it's possible. The reason I am is because I believe the big problem is not taxes, the big problem is spending."

— Milton Friedman, American economist*

$ettle the Discussion Questions

1. Did your education and upbringing teach you that the practices and policies of FDR's New Deal helped our economy? What are the ramifications for today if this is not true, and how did the New Deal policies actually hurt the economy?

2. What is at the root of consumer economics? What drives us to make purchases with money we do not have? How is this different from the driving force of *Godonomics*?

3. How was King Saul's rule different from God's rule over Israel? What were the effects of installing a king over Israel?

$tudy the $ummary $tatements

The question facing the Christian is often which king he will choose. In whom will he place his trust? We often place our trust in man-made governments to solve our problems and provide security. We ignore God's warning that strong and intrusive governments take away the liberty that is so vital to *Godonomics*. By trading liberty for security, we lose the freedom to manage our finances according to God's laws. Excessive man-made governments consume our wealth and diminish our capability to invest and generously give to others. The moment we embrace man's devices is the moment we become less free and less prosperous. Limited government fosters a prosperous economy and frees us to manage our resources as we are led by God. Placing our faith in the King who sacrificed Himself for us is the first step in grasping the principles of *Godonomics*. By trusting the economic wisdom God gives us in Scripture, we can avoid being enslaved to debt and enjoy the freedom and prosperity King Jesus offers.

$how $upport

In 1 Samuel 8:6–20, God uses Samuel to forewarn the people about the problems with looking to an earthly king and expanding the role of government. Circle how many times the phrases "his" and "yours" are used. Then underline the number of times Samuel warns that the "king will take."

* www.rightwingnews.com/interviews/an-interview-with-milton-friedman-2/

1 Samuel 8:6–20

But the thing displeased Samuel when they said, "Give us a king to judge us." So Samuel prayed to the LORD. And the LORD said to Samuel, "Heed the voice of the people in all that they say to you; for they have not rejected you, but they have rejected Me, that I should not reign over them. According to all the works which they have done since the day that I brought them up out of Egypt, even to this day — with which they have forsaken Me and served other gods — so they are doing to you also. Now therefore, heed their voice. However, you shall solemnly forewarn them, and show them the behavior of the king who will reign over them.

So Samuel told all the words of the LORD to the people who asked him for a king. And he said, "This will be the behavior of the king who will reign over you: He will take your sons and appoint them for his own chariots and to be his horsemen, and some will run before his chariots. He will appoint captains over his thousands and captains over his fifties, will set some to plow his ground and reap his harvest, and some to make his weapons of war and equipment for his chariots. He will take your daughters to be perfumers, cooks, and bakers. And he will take the best of your fields, your vineyards, and your olive groves, and give them to his servants. He will take a tenth of your grain and your vintage, and give it to his officers and servants. And he will take your male servants, your female servants, your finest young men, and your donkeys, and put them to his work. He will take a tenth of your sheep. And you will be his servants. And you will cry out in that day because of your king whom you have chosen for yourselves, and the LORD will not hear you in that day."

Nevertheless the people refused to obey the voice of Samuel; and they said, "No, but we will have a king over us, that we also may be like all the nations, and that our king may judge us and go out before us and fight our battles."

$cripture to $avor

Proverbs 13:22

A good man leaves an inheritance to his children's children, but the wealth of the sinner is stored up for the righteous.

Deuteronomy 28:44

He shall lend to you, but you shall not lend to him; he shall be the head, and you shall be the tail.

"So . . . What Would God Say to FDR?"

Stop spending tomorrow's money today!

— God

Soak in the Sure Sayings

"With the exception only of the period of the gold standard, practically all governments of history have used their exclusive power to issue money to defraud and plunder the people."

— Friedrich A. Hayek*

Introduction

In our fourth session, "What Would God Say to Alan Greenspan?" we'll investigate three illusions — the illusion of value, the illusion of abundance, and the illusion of generosity. We'll gain an understanding of the true meaning of inflation, the cause of rising prices, the cause of home devaluation, and the cause of our economic crash.

If someone came into your house and over time slowly stole more than half of your possessions, would you want to know who did it and how they did it? Do you wonder what caused your house to drop in price 20, 30, 40, or even 50 percent? This session demonstrates how our dollars have been robbed of their buying power by 90 percent over the past 100 years.

Do you consider yourself a generous or a greedy person? Plunge into this session to evaluate what type of standard we are using for that determination.

Do you ever wonder if God really cares about money and the economy? Let's gain insight from God's instructions in the Book of Proverbs on the importance He places on sound money rather than dishonest scales!

Luke 12:16-21

Then He spoke a parable to them, saying: "The ground of a certain rich man yielded plentifully. And he thought within himself, saying, 'What shall I do, since I have no room to store my crops?' So he said, 'I will do this: I will pull down my barns and build greater, and there I will store all my crops and my goods. And I will say to my soul, "Soul, you have many goods laid up for many years; take your ease; eat, drink, and be merry." ' But God said to him, 'Fool! This night your soul will be required of you; then whose will those things be which you have provided?' So is he who lays up treasure for himself, and is not rich toward God."

$hare in Prayer

$ee the Godly Perspective

Think about it — how stable can an economy truly be, if the stability of the currency is not based on an asset such as gold or oil, but is rather based on the promise of good financial management? Most paper currencies are based solely on that promise alone. Our government has so poorly managed our money with overspending and excessive borrowing that we are up to 22 trillion dollars in debt. Would the God who always backs up His promises with real wealth be pleased with a system of empty promises? Can anyone truly be wealthy and secure in their property and resources when it is all based on paper promises? God demands sound money, just weights, and fair scales!

* *Choice in Currency*: A Way to Stop Inflation; Friedrich August Hayek, Ivor F. Peace; Institute of Economic Affairs: 1976; www. adamsmith.org

$earch for Truth

We now come to the point in this series where a primary mechanism of consumer economics is revealed. Watch for three financial illusions by which humans are prone to be duped in their finances. Glean a new understanding of the role the Federal Reserve System plays in our economy when they print fiat money — paper currency backed by nothing of any real value. Notice how the Federal Reserve System, a privately owned banking institution, creates the illusion of a booming economy by lowering interest rates, resulting in devalued but abundant cash. This false economy would not be such a powerful, enslaving mechanism were it not for our tendency toward a problem with which every human being struggles. With *Godonomics*, learn how to unmask these three illusions impressed upon us by ourselves, as well as by others!

$tart the DVD $ession

(32 minutes)

Illusion #1:

The Illusion of 1. _____

Micah 6:11

Shall I acquit someone with dishonest scales, with a bag of false weights? (NIV)

2. The illusion of value comes from _____ scales.

3. The value of money used to be tied to a _____. In America, the commodity was gold.

4. When President Woodrow Wilson wanted to print more money without getting more gold, he exchanged the commodity of gold for a _____ to make good economic decisions.

The 5. _____ 6. _____ steals our money without the public ever knowing it, or ever realizing the scales have been changed.

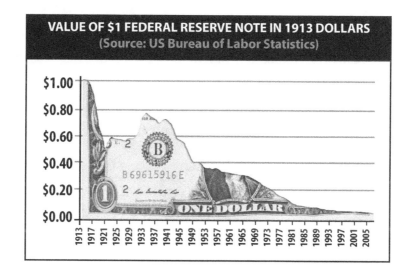

VALUE OF $1 FEDERAL RESERVE NOTE IN 1913 DOLLARS
(Source: US Bureau of Labor Statistics)

Proverbs 11:1

Dishonest scales are an abomination to the LORD, but a just weight is His delight.

Deuteronomy 25:15

If you weigh and measure things honestly, the LORD your God will let you enjoy a long life in the land he is giving you (CEV).

7. God cares about _____.

8. According to Keynesian economics, "prices going up" is _____.

9. Austrian economists note that rising prices is not inflation — inflation _____ in higher prices.

10. The Federal Reserve printed more money and therefore _____ the dollar.

Proverbs 14:31

He who oppresses the poor reproaches his Maker, but he who honors Him has mercy on the needy.

Proverbs 11:14

"Where there is no counsel, the people fall: but in the multitude of counselors there is safety."

For Further Study: Go to the government website at the Bureau of Labor Statistics and check it out for yourself. If you put in 100 dollars of 1913 bills, what could they be worth today? Or said differently, what could they buy today? The calculator will tell you how much buying power has been stolen through inflation, the devaluing of the dollar. http://www.bls.gov/data/inflation_calculator.htm.

Illusion #2:
The Illusion of 11. _____

Luke 12:15

And He said to them, "Take heed, and beware of covetousness, for one's life does not consist in the abundance of the things he possesses."

The Faces of Greed include:
12. _____
13. _____
14. _____
15. _____
16. _____

Luke 21:1–4

And He looked up and saw the rich putting their gifts into the treasury, and He saw also a certain poor widow putting in two mites. So He said, "Truly I say to you that this poor widow has put in more than all; for all these out of their abundance have put in offerings for God, but she out of her poverty put in all the livelihood that she had."

17. Everybody struggles with greed. The only wise thing to do is assume that you too struggle with

_____.

The reasons for greed often seem smart or legitimate, but the problem is being rich toward
18. _____, not toward 19. _____.

Illusion #3:

_____

The Illusion of 20. _____

21. The illusion of generosity means we measure or define generosity by our own _____ of what we are doing.

22. The average Christ follower gives away less than _____ percent of their income.

   Godonomics is not about giving out of your abundance, but rather about 23. _____ your life in such a way to produce, profit, and save so that you can be 24. _____ 25. _____ to others.

26. If we struggle with generosity, we need to look deeper into Jesus' _____ for us.

2 Corinthians 8:9

For you know the grace of our Lord Jesus Christ, that though He was rich, yet for your sakes He became poor, that you through His poverty might become rich.

$ettle the Discussion Questions

1. How does printing money we don't have to help the poor actually hurt the poor?

2. Why is "sound money," money that is tied to a commodity like gold, a fair and just economic principle for everyone?

3. What causes a housing bubble, and why does it fail to reflect real value?

$tudy the $ummary $tatements

Jesus gave His very best for us, and so we should for Him. How do we do that? The Bible tells us helping others is like giving to Him. The driving force of *Godonomics* is spending, investing, and giving, not just for ourselves, but for others.

In a consumer-based economy manipulated by private banks like the Federal Reserve, through which our wealth and financial security become unstable, generosity is more difficult for us. This is why God would tell Alan Greenspan and all other chairmen of the Federal Reserve to stop the presses! Stop devaluing our currency! Though we don't like to admit it, we are to blame, too. We all deal with greed on some level.

Like the widow who gave her last two mites, we should give our best to others as unto the Lord. We can raise our children to give generously in spite of the errors of others, while also teaching them the biblical way governments should approach economy. *Godonomics* reaches beyond governmental policies and personal budgeting capabilities. It reaches into the very heart and soul within us and teaches us the true spirit behind giving to the needs of others.

$how $upport

Choose one of the verses discussed in this session that has made you rethink your attitude toward finances and copy it below. List how you wish to apply this verse in your life.

Verse:

Application:

$cripture to $avor

Proverbs 20:23

Diverse weights are an abomination to the LORD, and dishonest scales are not good.

Micah 6:10–11

Are there yet the treasures of wickedness in the house of the wicked, and the short measure that is an abomination? Shall I count pure those with the wicked scales, and with the bag of deceitful weights?

"So . . . What Would God Say to Alan Greenspan?"

Stop the presses!

— God

Screen Out the Subtle Sayings

"Religion is the sign of the oppressed creature, the heart of a heartless world, and the soul of soulless conditions. It is the opium of the people. . . .Revolutions are the locomotives of history."

— Karl Marx*

Introduction

In Session Five, "What Would God Say to Karl Marx?" we'll grapple with three important aspects of a national economy and how they impact our individual lives: the scale, the purchase, and the worldview. God's principles of liberty, prosperity, and generosity are in complete contradiction to the teachings of Karl Marx and communism. Looking through these two views, we'll find out how individuals, cities, and nations go from being prosperous to bankrupt!

How can we vote in such a way to keep prosperity a vital part of the future? This session will give us two tests that will allow us to size up a politician in either party and understand their basic view on economics in less than five minutes. We'll also be able to explain why and where the government is wasting our money and what we can do about it. Understanding first-party, second-party, and third-party purchases will give us a more complete foundation for discerning why government purchases are always third-party purchases that waste the taxpayer's money.

Finally, we'll compare the American Revolution's proclamation for <u>life</u>, <u>liberty</u>, and the <u>pursuit of happiness</u> with the French Revolution's cry for <u>liberty</u>, <u>fraternity</u>, and <u>equality</u>. We'll also review why the inalienable rights from our Creator were paramount in our Constitution! Let's learn what God would say to Karl Marx!

$hare in Prayer

$ee the Godly Perspective

God's greatest gift to us is freedom — freedom to choose — freedom to make mistakes. We can try to make ourselves prosperous, or trust the government to provide prosperity for us. The end result of both is the same: failure. True freedom and prosperity come from God as we practice His principles. Throughout Scripture, God has warned us that trusting in men, whether ourselves or governments, is not the answer. We should trust in God and His principles for freedom and prosperity. The Truth can then set us free.

$earch for Truth

In Session Five, we'll study three aspects of a national economy: the scale, the purchase, and the worldview. Looking at these through the eyes of Karl Marx and the system that has come to bear his name, we see Karl Marx teaching that government can solve society's problems. No, Marx didn't put it quite that way, but if we watch closely, we will see how the principles of socialism keep coming back to that basic assumption. Note how American history has exposed the fallacies of socialistic promises.

Dare to compare humanism with God's standards. Dare to look at the real differences between the American Revolution and the French Revolution. Discover the underlying secret to prosperity — both for an individual and for a nation.

* *The Class Struggles in France* (1848-1850), Karl Marx, International Publishers: 1935; *Critique of Hegel's 'Philosophy of Right'*, Karl Marx, University Press: 1970

$tart the DVD $ession

(34 minutes)

(34 minutes)

Karl Marx said he came to offer 1. _____. In reality, Karl Marx offered a system in which he would have 2. _____ 3. _____. This stands in stark contrast to what we have been studying in *Godonomics*. God wants us to experience liberty, prosperity, and generosity.

4. Four percent of the world has produced the most playwrights, the most inventions, and the biggest economic gains — _____!

5. Fifty percent of the world lives on _____ dollars a day or less.

6. Generosity can be traced back to the incredible _____ of America.

7. Arkansas's Gross Domestic Product (GDP) is higher than the _____ largest nation in the world, Pakistan.

8. Louisiana's GDP is higher than the _____ largest nation in the world, Indonesia.

9. The GDP of the entire nation of Russia is less than that of _____.

10. In America, liberty has led to _____, which has led to generosity.

11. The story of _____ has always been a part of Jesus' story.

Three Aspects of *Godonomics*:

Aspect #1: 13. _____

When someone takes away a percentage of your income, two things happen. You have less 14. _____ and lower 15. _____.

16. Someone who works all day long but gets to take home none of his or her income is called a _____.

17. We can evaluate the trajectory of a world leader by looking to see if he is moving the taxation scale of a nation toward more _____ or more slavery.

The economy of every nation throughout history has demonstrated that the greater the freedom, the greater the 18. _____, and the greater the government, the greater the 19. _____.

20. Under _____, tax dollars are funneled through an inefficient and often corrupt organization, and are not efficiently spent.

21. At one point, Detroit, Michigan, was the _____ city in America. Due to heavy taxation, out of the 26 largest cities in America, it is now the poorest.

22. A case study of North Korea and South Korea clearly demonstrates how the scale works. In North Korea, 2.5 million people starve each year. In South Korea, her economy boasts the _____ largest GDP in the world.

23. Government doesn't produce; it _____, enslaving us along the way.

Taxation Scale:

Percent the Producer Keeps

Aspect #2: 24. _____

First-party purchases have two determining variables.

25. _____

26. _____

27. _____ purchases: I pay for something with my money to provide services or products for myself.

In a free society, there is no such thing as an 28. _____ 29. _____,
as long as the consumer is free to choose.

30. _____ purchases: I pay for something with someone else's money to provide services or
products for myself. Or I pay for something with my money for services or products for someone else.

31. _____ purchases: I pay for something with someone else's money for services or
products for someone else.

32. All government purchases are _____ purchases.

33. Communist and Socialist countries build walls in order to keep their people in, so that the people might
"_____"!

That's why President Reagan said, "34. _____ 35. _____ that wall!"

Mark 8:35

For whoever desires to save his life will lose it, but whoever loses his life for My sake and the gospel's
will save it.

James 2:8

If you really fulfill the royal law according to the Scripture, "You shall love your neighbor as
yourself," you do well.

36. The more you _____ others, the more you receive!

Aspect #3: 37. _____

These two views of life impact how you view policies, responsibility, and problem-solving.

Humanism

Man is good.

Man's environment is responsible for his behavior.

Man is the standard.

Rights are granted by the group.

God's Worldview

God is good, and man is in need of a Savior.

Man's environment is not responsible for his behavior; rather, the individual is responsible for his own behavior.

God is the standard.

Rights are granted by God.

Romans 3:23

For all have sinned, and fall short of the glory of God.

Romans 5:8

But God demonstrates His own love toward us, in that while we were still sinners, Christ died for us.

Romans 6:23

For the wages of sin is death, but the gift of God is eternal life in Christ Jesus our Lord.

38. The environment is not responsible for my problems: I, _____, am responsible.

Declaration of Independence: "We hold these truths to be self-evident, that all men are created equal, that they are endowed by their Creator with certain unalienable Rights, that among these are 39. _____, 40. _____ and the pursuit of 41. _____ (originally – 42. _____). That to secure these rights, Governments are instituted among Men, deriving their just powers from the consent of the governed."

43. The _____ became the motivating symbol to persuade Frenchmen to become a part of the new group and the new equality, because their rights did not come from God. Their rights came from the Fraternity.

Ben Franklin's speech imploring his fellow countrymen to pray for wisdom while forming the Constitution:

"Mr. President, The small progress we have made after four or five weeks close attendance and continual reasonings with each other — our different sentiments on almost every question, several of the last producing as many noes as ays, is me thinks a melancholy proof of the imperfection of the Human Understanding. We indeed seem to feel our own want of political wisdom, since we have been running about in search of it. We have gone back to ancient history for models of Government, and examined the different forms of those Republics which having been formed with the seeds of their own dissolution, now no longer exist. And we have viewed Modern States all round Europe, but find none of their Constitutions suitable to our circumstances.

In this situation of this Assembly, groping as it were in the dark to find political truth, and scarce able to distinguish it when presented to us, how has it happened, Sir, that we have not hitherto once thought of humbly applying to the Father of lights to illuminate our understandings? In the beginning of the Contest with Great Britain, when we were sensible of danger, we had daily prayer in this room for the Divine protection. Our prayers, Sir, were heard, and they were graciously answered. All of us who were engaged in the struggle must have observed frequent instances of a superintending providence in our favor. To that kind providence we owe this happy opportunity of consulting in peace on the means of establishing our future national felicity. And have we now forgotten that powerful friend? Or do we imagine that we no longer need his assistance? I have lived, Sir, a long time, and the longer I live, the more convincing proofs I see of this truth — that God governs in the affairs of men. And if a sparrow cannot fall to the ground without his notice, is it probable that an empire can rise without his aid? We have been assured, Sir, in the Sacred Writings, that 'except the Lord build the house they labor in vain that build it.' I firmly believe this; and I also believe that without his concurring aid, we shall succeed in this political building no better than the Builders of Babel. I therefore move that prayers imploring the assistance of Heaven and its blessing on our deliberation be held in this assembly every morning before we proceed to business."

The First Continental Congress then took three days for 44. _____, 45. _____, and 46. _____ before coming back together as a group. Six weeks later, they had penned the Constitution of the United States of America.

Our inherent dignity and our inherent value does not come from the group. It comes from "creation ex deo" — created by the Heavenly Father.

God 47. wants to 48. _____ us to come back to Him, both individually and as a _____.

$ettle the Discussion Questions

1. Read Proverbs 24:3–4. How do the principles of price and quality affect purchasing and investing? How do they motivate us to be wise and frugal in our financial choices?

2. What is a First-Party Purchase, and how is it different from a Third-Party Purchase?

3. Compare/contrast the three ideals of the French Revolution to the three enshrined in the American Declaration of Independence.

Finally, Americans changed the order of the ideals, carefully and purposefully putting life ahead of liberty and happiness. Only when a nation truly respects and protects the sanctity of life can it enjoy liberty and the pursuit of happiness.

$tudy the $ummary $tatements

It's all connected. Like a string of upset dominoes, the compromise of the individual on these issues will rock the nation to its very core. When men and families no longer humble themselves before God, seeking to implement His ways in all aspects of their lives — including finances and principles of government — then the community is weakened. They elect mayors, councilmen, state representatives, and eventually congressmen, senators, and presidents who do not acknowledge God or the principles of *Godonomics*. The resulting departure from scriptural principles of fairness, frugality, brotherly kindness, limited government, free enterprise, and sound money then leads the whole nation into poverty and slavery. Like the indicator on the Taxation Scale, a nation will either sway toward freedom and prosperity, or toward more government intervention, increased taxes, less individual responsibility, less freedom, and less wealth beginning with the actions of the individuals who make up the nation. As Scripture bears out, when men leave God's governance, they are delivered over to governmental oppression. When they return to God, the Lord gives them freedom, which naturally results in the blessings and prosperity of God.

$how $upport

List one "upset domino" in the chain of your life that you will reset this week to move your family toward a more Godonomic perspective. Some ideas would include: memorize a Scripture; invest the time to educate another American on the benefits of Godonomic principles; make a specific change in how you will make your first-party, second-party, or third-party purchases.

Evaluate where your family is on the Historical Cycle of Nations. If you are already in the "Prosperous Cycle," list at least one action you will undertake this week in order to help protect your family from falling into the "Apathy Cycle." If you are not in the "Prosperous Cycle," list at least one action you will undertake this week to begin moving your family to that place of God's blessing.

$cripture to $avor

Leviticus 25:10

And you shall consecrate the fiftieth year, and proclaim liberty throughout all the land to all its inhabitants.

2 Corinthians 3:17

Now the Lord is the Spirit; and where the Spirit of the Lord is, there is liberty.

"So . . . What Would God Say to Karl Marx?"

Get a barber and stop taking away people's freedom!

— God

Soak in the Sure Sayings

"The problem with socialism is that you eventually run out of other people's money."
— Margaret Thatcher*

Introduction

In this sixth session of *Godonomics*, we'll enhance our understanding of taxes, of coercion, and of the joy of individual generosity. This section shows how God's principles and common sense economic policies actually help the economy. We'll look at how both John F. Kennedy and Ronald Reagan's lower tax rates actually increased tax revenue. If you have wondered why companies today are shedding jobs and why states have to dramatically slash budgets, this chapter will help you grasp the relationship between taxation and employment.

We'll discover different types of giving and how they affect our hearts. What type of motivation for giving fills you with guilt, pride, or fear? Which type of giving fills you with peace, contentment, and true joy? God has a lot to say about submission — including paying taxes. However, God also warns us against pursuing excessive government that overtaxes its people and spends the revenue in wasteful ways. We will again visit the subjects of individualism versus collectivism, as clearly taught in the Scriptures, in relation to giving. Yes — *Godonomics* (what God has to say about economy and money) has a lot to say to the I.R.S.!

2 Corinthians 9:5–8

Therefore I thought it necessary to exhort the brethren to go to you ahead of time, and prepare your generous gift beforehand, which you had previously promised, that it may be ready as a matter of generosity and not as a grudging obligation. But this I say: He who sows sparingly will also reap sparingly, and he who sows bountifully will also reap bountifully. So let each one give as he purposes in his heart, not grudgingly or of necessity; for God loves a cheerful giver. And God is able to make all grace abound toward you, that you, always having all sufficiency in all things, may have an abundance for every good work.

2 Corinthians 8:9

For you know the grace of our Lord Jesus Christ, that though He was rich, yet for your sakes He became poor, that you through His poverty might become rich.

$hare in Prayer

$ee the Godly Perspective

If we were required to give a specific amount to a charity about which we cared absolutely nothing, would we give any more than the required amount? Probably not. This is a coercive approach, which forces us to give to causes and programs about which we don't care or necessarily approve. Begrudging giving is the result. This type of giving is not God's way.

But what if we were required to give to a charity about which we were passionate, and we were given the opportunity to give of our own free will? We would probably give more abundantly because we would be

* (Widely used paraphrase of a quote from a 1976 television interview with former British prime minister Margaret Thatcher.)

giving out of a cheerful heart. That's *Godonomics*! God clearly instructs us to give individually and to give cheerfully out of a grateful heart.

$earch for Truth

To Give: to relinquish; to yield; to proffer to another; to deliver; to make gifts or donations; not keeping for oneself. Notice in this session the three primary ways giving can take place. Two of them involve coercion. Only one comes from the grace of God. *Godonomics* giving is motivated by thankfulness to God and a desire to pass along the grace bestowed on us. Government doesn't afford us this type of giving. Notice how neither major party in the American political system differs on this. While they may differ on how to coerce giving, neither abandon the concept of coercion itself.

Coercion is exercised by religious organizations also. In fact, this session reveals that many religious methods of coercion through fear and deceit are the same as the ones used by corrupt governments and politicians. Once again, listen for the stark contrast of *Godonomics* versus coercion on the subject of giving!

Discover what the Laffer Curve is, and how it affects taxation and revenue. Can <u>lower taxes</u> actually <u>increase government revenue</u>? Follow history and see!

$tart the DVD $ession

(28 minutes)

2 Corinthians 9:5–8

Therefore I thought it necessary to exhort the brethren to go to you ahead of time, and prepare your generous gift beforehand, which you had previously promised, that it may be ready as a matter of generosity and not as a grudging obligation. But this I say: He who sows sparingly will also reap sparingly, and he who sows bountifully will also reap bountifully. So let each one give as he purposes in his heart, not grudgingly or of necessity; for God loves a cheerful giver. And God is able to make all grace abound toward you, that you, always having all sufficiency in all things, may have an abundance for every good work.

There are two types of coercion: 1. _____ and 2. _____ coercion.

3. Coercive giving makes us more and more _____, rather than more and more cheerful.

History of the IRS

1787 — U.S. Constitution prohibited a "direct" federal tax

1862 — "Revenue tax" levied on incomes to finance the Union during the Civil War

1895 — Supreme Court made Income tax unconstitutional

1913 — Income tax of 1 percent levied on only the top 1 percent of producers (invoked by President Woodrow Wilson)

1943 — Withholding tax from paychecks invoked as an emergency effort to finance World War II

4. _____ does not align with the Democrats nor the Republicans, but rather is a whole new way of thinking about money and economics.

Romans 13:7

"Render therefore to all their due: taxes to whom taxes are due."

Matthew 22:17, 22:21

"Teacher, what do You think? Is it lawful to pay taxes to Caesar, or not?" "Render therefore to Caesar the things that are Caesar's, and to God the things that are God's."

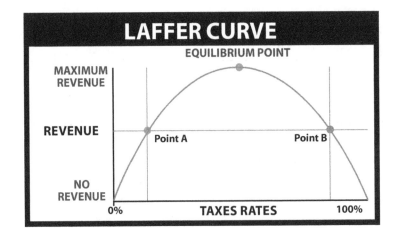

LAFFER CURVE

EQUILIBRIUM POINT

MAXIMUM REVENUE

REVENUE

Point A   Point B

NO REVENUE

0%   TAXES RATES   100%

"5. _____ rates of taxation will 6. _____ economic activity and so raise the levels of personal and corporate income as to yield within a few years an 7. _____ flow of revenues to the federal government."

The Laffer Curve shows that the 8. _____ 9. _____ go up, the 10. _____ 11. _____ you get.

12. President Franklin D. Roosevelt said that "the forgotten man" was the _____.

As illustrated in *The Forgotten Man* by Amity Shlaes, political coercion takes place when people are forced to give to those in need.

13. Amity Shlaes correctly demonstrates that the real forgotten man is the _____.

If someone is in need and we have extra, we should 14. _____ to that person, but government should not 15. _____ /16. _____ us to do so through taxation.

17. Religious _____

Guilt — Fear — Pride

These produce begrudging giving, attempt to manipulate God, and falsely assume that all God's blessings are materialistic.

18. Giving _____

- Given without any attempt to make up for our sins
- Given with motivation of a grateful heart for God's grace
- Given with a confidence in God's promised provision for our needs
- Given as seeds to invest in God's work
- Given in response to what Christ gave for us, becoming poor that he might make us rich

Paul says that 19. _____ is the 20. _____.

God gave us the means to 21. _____ so we should 22. _____ our profits to give and to invest that we might glorify Him.

In our study of *Godonomics* we will have learned that socialism 23. _____ 24. _____, and that capitalism doesn't eliminate 25. _____, but it does neutralize it.

God's principles for economy will make you:

- More 26. _____
- More 27. _____
- More 28. _____

$ettle the Discussion Questions

What was your favorite holiday growing up, or your favorite holiday now? Does it involve giving? What emotion does giving freely provide for you? When we give freely out of love, gratitude, or concern for others, we are obeying *Godonomics'* giving principles. Obeying God's plan reaps many rewards — emotionally, spiritually, and financially.

1. What are ways that religion can use coercion to bring about giving?

2. Explain one way lowering taxes might result in increased tax revenue.

3. Discuss F.D.R.'s Forgotten Man concept. How is coerced giving of this sort contrary to *Godonomics*? What is the difference between the U.S. political parties as it pertains to this error?

$tudy the $ummary $tatements

So, what can I do? You might be asking yourself this question now that you understand that government is not following God's laws of economics. *Godonomics* is not a magic formula for governments. *Godonomics* is a set of biblical principles that every individual can live by, inspire others to live by, and encourage their leaders to live by. Think of the good God has done for us, and how He wants us to give out of our gratitude for these gifts. Rather than go along with the mentality of giving only what is required, embrace the Christian ideal of going the extra mile. Invest in others. Give to worthy ministries that are sharing God's gift with others.

Let's not get caught up in consumer economics, which puts consuming before producing, enslaving ourselves to debt because we "deserve" something we can't afford. Rather, let's manage our finances in accordance with the system of *Godonomics*: produce, then profit, then save; and then give, spend, and invest. The result? God's liberty, prosperity, and generosity!

$how $upport

What would God say to you?

Give of a cheerful heart, and it shall be given to you pressed down, shaken together, and running over.

Luke 6:38

Give, and it will be given to you: good measure, pressed down, shaken together, and running over will be put into your bosom. For with the same measure that you use, it will be measured back to you.

$cripture to $avor

2 Corinthians 9:7

So let each one give as he purposes in his heart, not grudgingly or of necessity; for God loves a cheerful giver.

"So . . . What Would God Say to the I.R.S.?"

Stop coercing people to give!

— God

You can't grant people true liberty without the foundation of My Word.

— God

Let's Save!

The Plan

Set a goal to save a set amount of money by a certain time. Write your goal here:

Once you have reached your goal, what do you plan to do with your savings? Will you hang onto it for a long-term goal such as a car or college? Will you purchase something you have wanted for a while? Write your plan here:

How will you earn the money to save? Think of some revenue streams you can explore like chores, selling something, etc. Write your plan here:

How did you do?

Did you reach your goals? What did you do with your savings? What did you learn from this exercise? Will you continue to save?

"The habit of thinking about work as something simply done for money is so ingrained in our society that it is hard to think about work done for the sake of the work itself.

....'Doctors practice medicine not primarily to relieve suffering, but to make a living, the patients' cure is something that happens along the way.

Lawyers accept briefs not because they have a passion for justice, but because the law enables them to live.

During WWII, people were drawn into an army and found a new surprising sense of fulfillment in their work.'

For the first time in their lives, they found themselves doing something, not for the pay, but for the sake of getting the thing done."

— Dorothy Sayers*

Introduction

Note to Students: The video sessions in this part of the course address leaders, business owners, and CEOs. Students can be leaders in their churches, schools, families, and among friends. You will also learn about business, economics, and leadership. Apply what you are learning to your life right now and also store it up to be used in your future career and callings.

What would happen if you really knew your work was part of a much bigger plan and purpose? What if the CEO of your company or chairman of your board sent you on assignment for the month doing something different than usual, but you were handpicked for the assignment by the head of your industry? Further, what if the CEO told you that you were representing him in disguise, managing, working, and providing for others on his behalf? As Pastor Tim Keller noted when introducing some of Martin Luther's theology in reference to work, "God doesn't have to do it that way but He is. He's loving you through other people's work. And he's loving others through your work. He goes as far as to say that the baker and the farmer in work is God in disguise. These are the masks of God. God is loving you and distributing His gifts through work." The CEO of the universe wants to bless all of creation by asking you to go on assignment for him in work.**

Jesus says that God strategically places us in the world to make a difference. And when we realize that, we begin to whistle while we work. In His Sermon on the Mount, He uses the words "set" and "place" when speaking about how God places people in different places in the world.

Read Proverbs 31

$tart the DVD $ession 7

(30 minutes)

---

* *Letters to a Diminished Church: Passionate Arguments for the Relevance of Christian Doctrine*; Dorothy L. Sayers; W Publishing Group: 2004. pgs. 66, 125.

** Pastor Tim Keller, www.christianpost.com/news/tim-keller-spiritual-and-secular-jobs-are-gods-work-48754/

1. Capitalism is not just a good idea; it's _____ idea.

1 Corinthians 7:17–20

"But as God has distributed to each one, as the Lord has called each one, so let him walk. . . . Let each one remain in the same calling in which he was called."

2. Paul is addressing a group who has recently heard and explored Christ and are in differing places in career and industry in the metropolis of Corinth. He says, don't change careers now that you are a Christ follower, God has "distributed you" and "_____ you" into that industry to "wear His mask." So Paul speaks of calling and being distributed strategically by God in the context of work in the hopes that you and I learn to whistle while we work.

3. Climb the _____ ladder instead of the corporate ladder.

4. Meaning and _____ increases as we move up the ladder.

There are four stages to the ladder of work. There are four steps on the ladder to meaning and success:

5. First Step: Work for 9. _____

6. Second Step: Work for 8. _____

7. Third Step: Work for 7. _____

8. Fourth Step: Work for 6. _____

9. _____ celebrates work and profiting.

10. _____ designed us with self-interest, the desire to work and make a difference. In fact, self-interest is key to the first stage of work.

11. Jesus references self-interest when He says the whole law is summed up in this, "Love your neighbor as _____."

12. God honors our _____, to work, and we begin to find 13. _____ and that God makes us 14. _____ to impacr other people.

15. 2 Thessalonians 3:10: "If you don't work, you don't _____" (The Message).

1 Corinthians 9:7–10

Whoever goes to war at his own expense? Who plants a vineyard and does not eat of its fruit? Or who tends a flock and does not drink of the milk of the flock? Do I say these things as a mere man? Or does not the law say the same also? For it is written in the law of Moses, "You shall not muzzle an ox while it treads out the grain." Is it oxen God is concerned about? Or does He say it altogether for our sakes? For our sakes, no doubt, this is written, that he who plows should plow in hope.

16. The first step of climbing the portrait ladder is _____ work.

17. Second step: work for _____. (a career)

The next step is where you move from a 18. _____ to a 19. _____, and you begin to 20. _____ others through your work.

Proverbs 31: "She profits" — "discerns her merchandise is good." Our business owner discerned her merchandise was good knowing that she would buy it at this price and quality. So would her customers. She sold grapes and high-end expensive clothes. Fashioning and shaping were ways she was imitating her creative God.

Worldview Note: While other religions and philosophies taught that matter was inherently evil, like Greek dualism, the Bible taught that the God of creation reached His hands into the dirt of creation and "fashioned" it into something productive, beautiful, and good. This idea was so powerful that Christ-followers know that when we reach into the commodities of the world, and fashion them into art, service, widgets, and products, we are doing something inherently godly by imitating our creative Creator. Therefore, work is a spiritual act reflecting our purpose. And just as God the Creator fashioned us so that we could experience His joy, love, peace, and wonder . . . it was an "others-centered creative product desiring to share joy with others." So too, the move from step 1 to step 2 in work is the process of moving from working for self . . . to working for others.

21. Third step: work for _____ (a calling).

22. You need step 1 and 2 to create the money, profit, and influence to _____ the world.

23. Money is not unproductive or wrong. The Greek idea of _____ taught that the world was inherently bad, that matter was bad.

24. "Vocation" comes from the Latin word *vocare* which means to call. A vocation is a _____.

All of life can be a 25. _____ act of 26. _____.

27. Fourth step: work for _____ (purpose).

God has you in the world for a 28. _____ and a bigger 29. _____.

Colossians 3:17

And whatever you do in word or deed, do all in the name of the Lord Jesus, giving thanks to God the Father through Him.

Ephesians 6:7–8

. . . with goodwill doing service, as to the Lord, and not to men, knowing that whatever good anyone does, he will receive the same from the Lord, whether he is a slave or free.

30. We represent God in our work by wearing His _____.

$ettle the Discussion Question

1. God gives us all capital (talents, skills, opportunities, passions) and He offers us freedom to use that capital for His purposes. And He paints a portrait of work that is very fulfilling. It's not a corporate ladder, it's a portrait ladder of higher, others-centered living. It's God's idea to use His capital to bless others. There are four steps: work for self, work for customer, work for society, work for God. Climb the Portrait Ladder rather than the Corporate Ladder — it's better up there. Which step are you missing? Which step do you need to start working on?

$how $upport

The step from career to calling is significant and one that many men and women have made. There is a book called *Halftime* that challenges people in this stage to move from career to calling, to take this next step. There is an interview with a guy who did just that. Listen to his story: Search online (with parent's permission) for it.

$tudy the $ummary

Step 1 is a paycheck: working for self

Step 2 is a career: working for customers

Step 3 is a calling: working for a society

Step 4 is a purpose: working for our Creator

"If lay people cannot find any spiritual meaning in their work, they are condemned to live a certain dual life; not connecting what they do on Sunday morning with what they do the rest of the week. They need to discover that the very actions of daily life are spiritual and enable people to touch God in the world, not away from it. Such spirituality will say, 'Your work is your prayer.' "

— William Diehl*

Introduction

As many employers have noted, the mindset of Millennials is different. They don't celebrate 60-hour work weeks; they don't have the same "get out of my parents' house and prove myself" mindset. While Boomers and Gen-Xers go to their office and "get 'er done," Millennials love collaboration and working in teams. These generational differences celebrate different things and replicate different things.

We replicate what we celebrate.

Why do we replicate "yes men" in organizations? Because the awards we give out often go to people who said what was supposed to be said, right? Why do we replicate worn-out systems that don't challenge the status quo? Because we celebrate safe, tried and true systems, rather than well-measured but tested new ideas. Why do we replicate college students who tend to come out of college demonizing business and profit? Because they spent four years seeing an anti-business, anti-profit mindset being celebrated.

How does the Bible feel about profits, rewards, and entrepreneurship?

To listen to most pastors, you'd think business and profit are amoral at best, unless you give that money to the Church or ministry, right?

- If we demonize profits, should we be surprised that we get irresponsibility and a feeling of deserving entitlement?

- If we celebrate profits, progress, efforts, and reward them, we will replicate the same traits in our kids, family, and organization.

- If we celebrate "character qualities," we will replicate them in our organization.

* *Every Good Endeavor: Connecting Your Work to God's Work,* Timothy Keller; Dutton Publishing: 2012

Review Proverbs 31

The words of King Lemuel, the utterance which his mother taught him:

What, my son?

And what, son of my womb?

And what, son of my vows?

Do not give your strength to women,

Nor your ways to that which destroys kings.

It is not for kings, O Lemuel,

It is not for kings to drink wine,

Nor for princes intoxicating drink;

Lest they drink and forget the law,

And pervert the justice of all the afflicted.

Give strong drink to him who is perishing,

And wine to those who are bitter of heart.

Let him drink and forget his poverty,

And remember his misery no more.

Open your mouth for the speechless,

In the cause of all who are appointed to die,

Open your mouth, judge righteously,

And plead the cause of the poor and needy.

Whon can find a virtuous wife?

For her worth is far above rubies.

The heart of her husband safely trusts her;

So he will have no lack of gain.

She does him good and not evil

All the days of her life.

She seeks wool and flax,

And willingly works with her hands.

She is like the merchant ships,

She brings her food from afar.

She also rises while it is yet night,

And provides food for her household,

And a portion for her maidservants.

She considers a field and buys it;

From her profits she plants a vineyard.

She girds herself with strength,

And strengthens her arms.

She perceives that her merchandise is good,

And her lamp does not go out by night.

She stretches out her hands to the distaff,

And her hand holds the spindle.

She extends her hand to the poor,

Yes, she reaches out her hands to the needy.

She is not afraid of snow for her household,

For all her household is clothed with scarlet.

She makes tapestry for herself;

Her clothing is fine linen and purple.

Her husband is known in the gates,

When he sits among the elders of the land.

She makes linen garments and sells them,

And supplies sashes for the merchants.

Strength and honor are her clothing;

She shall rejoice in time to come.

She opens her mouth with wisdom,

And on her tongue is the law of kindness.

She watches over the ways of her household,

And does not eat the bread of idleness.

Her children rise up and call her blessed;

Her husband also, and he praises her:

"Many daughters have done well,

But you excel them all."

Charm is deceitful and beauty is passing,

But a woman who fears the LORD, she shall be praised.

Give her of the fruit of her hands,

And let her own works praise her in the gates.

$tart the DVD $ession

(33 minutes)

1. Profits R Good, Profits R Not _____

When we celebrate both these aspects, we are able to enjoy our profits without being enslaved to them.

Proverbs 31 introduces us to a businesswoman who finds a field that produces and then she profits from it. The Bible esteems this as a good and great thing. "Profits R Good," especially when those profits come by "discerning your merchandise is good" and offering it with a price, quality, and expertise that blesses others.

Acts 16:11–14

Therefore, sailing from Troas, we ran a straight course to Samothrace, and the next day came to Neapolis, and from there to Philippi, which is the foremost city of that part of Macedonia, a colony. And we were staying in that city for some days. And on the Sabbath day we went out of the city to the riverside, where prayer was customarily made; and we sat down and spoke to the women who met there. Now a certain woman named Lydia heard us. She was a seller of purple from the city of Thyatira.

Lydia, a business woman in the ancient city of Philippi in the Bible, was a who's who in the city amongst high-end clothing sellers.

Lydia was a seller of purple cloth. And she was so competent at it that she influenced a major market in a major city. She was a person who profited from selling high-end purple clothes in one of the most influential cities in Macedonia. The Bible celebrates this woman. In fact, as she began to explore Christ, God used her network of relationships and clients to allow her new life change and faith to spread throughout the city. Her competence, excellence, business model, and work for God honored God.

2. Lydia celebrated Profits R Good because of her celebration of _____ as a seller.

3. Profiting honors God and inspires others. Doing your work with _____, whatever it is, honors God.

Not only does competence become a way we celebrate that Profits R Good, but excellence is another.

Proverbs 31:16–24

She considers a field and buys it; from her profits she plants a vineyard. . . . She perceives that her merchandise is good, and her lamp does not go out by night. . . . She extends her hand to the poor, yes, she reaches out her hands to the needy. . . . She makes tapestry for herself; her clothing is fine linen and purple. . . . She makes linen garments and sells them, and supplies sashes for the merchants.

The Proverbs 31 woman celebrates her profits as a producer, artist, manufacturer, seller, and merchant. Her 4. _____ and 5. _____ made her an honor to God and others.

6. The _____ celebrates work, purchasing, selling, and providing. She examines her grapes, works day and night, and uses her money to help the needy and provide for her family.

There are two ways we can celebrate that Profits R Good in our work toward God: We celebrate with

7. _____ and 8. _____ in our work toward God.

9. We can also celebrate that Profits R Good through _____.

So the Bible teaches that Profits R Good, but also that Profits R Not Enough. They are not the ultimate. They will not bring final and lasting meaning. Lydia found that to be true.

10. We replicate what we _____. That allows us to whistle while we profit. But while Profits R Good, Profits R Not Enough.

Acts 16:11–15

We . . . came to . . . Philippi, which is the foremost city. . . . And we were staying in that city for some days. And on the Sabbath day we went out of the city to the riverside, where prayer was customarily made; and we sat down and spoke to the women who met there. Now a certain woman named Lydia heard us. She was a seller of purple from the city of Thyatira, who worshiped God. The Lord opened her heart to heed the things spoken by Paul. And when she and her household were baptized, she begged us, saying, "If you have judged me to be faithful to the Lord, come to my house and stay." So she persuaded us.

Despite running a high-end, successful business in a major port city in Macedonia (Greece), she was exploring and seeking God. Notice the Bible describes her as someone who "worshiped God" (we might say it like this, "Lydia was a spiritual person, a God seeker, or a spiritual explorer"). But notice the next line says, "The Lord opened her heart." Though she worshiped God, was spiritual, and was successful, she needed more than just success and money. In fact, she also needed more than just "god." She needed to open her heart to "a specific God." Paul introduced her to Jesus as God. And she was baptized. She heard something from Paul that told her that though her business and money were good, Profits R Not Enough.

Following the way of Christ can allow you to affirm profits while realizing that Profits R Not Enough. Profits can't be the ultimate thing. Work is good, but not the ultimate thing. Jesus said it this way:

Mark 8:36–37

For what will it profit a man if he gains the whole world, and loses his own soul? Or what will a man give in exchange for his soul?

This idea of "what is a fair wage" or "fair price" has been pondered by many before us. In *Ethics*, Plato wrestled with how to determine a "just price." The work of both Aquinas and Calvin raised the issue of determining just price: "For a long time, scholars assumed that the medieval conception of the 'just price' involved calculations of cost of production and other such measurable factors, but this conception was actually a minority view. The mainstream position was that of St. Albertus Magnus (and others), who held that the just price corresponded to what 'goods are worth according to the estimation of the market at the time of sale.' Aquinas's point that a seller of grain, knowing that additional supplies are on their way, has no moral obligation to disclose this information to his customers (although it may be especially virtuous for him to do so)."[1]

So, what does that mean? It means the fair market value at the time of sale or hiring is the "just price." However, a Christian pays differently by saying, "Fair Market Plus the Golden Rule." How would I pay if I want to do unto others as I would have them do unto me? An entry-level job might pay X, and then a Christian says, "Is X fair? If I was them, with their experience and ability, would I feel it was fair?" A Christ-follower doesn't just duplicate the culture's "fair value" (though it's moral), he or she asks another question. He says, "How can I pay differently by combining the fair value and the golden rule?"

When Christians realize that profits are good, but not enough," they begin to 11. _____ differently and 12. _____ differently.

Real World Application

Hobby Lobby CEO David Green said, "We're Christians, and we run our business on Christian principles. I've always said that the first two goals of our business are 1) to run our business in harmony with God's laws, and 2) to focus on people more than money. And that's what we've tried to do. We close early so our employees can see their families at night. We keep our stores closed on Sundays, one of the week's biggest shopping days, so that our workers and their families can enjoy a day of rest. We believe that it is by God's grace that Hobby Lobby has endured, and he has blessed us and our employees. We've not only added jobs in a weak economy, we've also raised wages for the past four years in a row. Our full-time employees start at 80% above minimum wage."[2]

Not all companies should be closed on Sundays or do what they did, BUT, look at how he is thinking through how to do this in his business. He is "paying differently."

As a follower of Christ, you add in the 13. _____ 14. _____ value plus the 15. _____ 16. _____.

17. Profit Differently: Don't Suck Out All the _____

Ruth 2:1–2

There was a relative of Naomi's husband, a man of great wealth, of the family of Elimelech. His name was Boaz. So Ruth the Moabitess said to Naomi, "Please let me go to the field, and glean heads of grain after him in whose sight I may find favor."

The Bible celebrates Boaz, a man of "great wealth" who ran a successful business that was able to "save the town of Bethlehem" during difficult times of famine and drought by running a successful business that employed families. But he profited differently, too. Rather than extracting every amount of profit out of the field that he could, he practiced the "gleaning principle" by leaving the corners of the field for the poor to work and glean in.

---

1   Rodney Stark, *The Victory of Reason: How Christianity Led to Freedom, Capitalism, and Western Success* (New York: Random House, 2005).
2   David Green, "Christian Companies Can't Bow to Sinful Mandate," *USA Today*, 9/12/12, http://usatoday30.usatoday.com/news/opinion/forum/story/2012-09-12/hhs-mandate-birth-control-sue-hobby-lobby/57759226/1.

18. Instead of sucking out all the profits, he knew profits aren't _____, so he was able to be generous to those in need.

19. Francis Schaeffer was speaking to a group of Christian businessmen in the late 1970s about how to apply this gleaning principle. He challenged them to really think about how they paid and blessed employees. He suggested that instead of only paying the fair market wage to entry and middle-level employees to maximize profits — even if you used those profits to make healthy philanthropic gifts — it would be more powerful and a more attractive pattern to the world about the ethics of _____, if we gave away less from making more so we could pay our employees in a way that was higher than the world's standards.[3]

20. Enjoy profits without being _____ to them.

- Money is fuel for providing for your own family according to 1 Timothy 5:8: "But if anyone does not provide for his own, and especially for those of his household, he has denied the faith and is worse than an unbeliever."

- Money is fuel for giving to the poor and needy: "She extends her hand to the poor, Yes, she reaches out her hands to the needy" (Proverbs 31:20).

- Money is fuel to invest in other producing ventures in the world: "She considers a field and buys it; from her profits she plants a vineyard" (Proverbs 31:16).

That chair you are lounging in? Could you have made it for yourself? Well, I suppose so, if we mean just the chair! Perhaps you did in fact go out to buy the wood, the nails, the glue, the stuffing, the springs — and put it all together. But if by making the chair we mean assembling each part from scratch, that's quite another matter. How do we get, say, the wood? Go and fell a tree? But only after first making the tools for that, and putting together some kind of vehicle to haul the wood, and constructing a mill to do the lumber, and roads to drive on from place to place? In short, a lifetime or two to make one chair!

We are physically unable, it is obvious, to provide ourselves from scratch with the household goods we can now see from wherever you and I are sitting — to say nothing of building and furnishing the whole house.

Consider everything else that we can use every day and never really see. Who builds and maintains the roads and streets we take for granted? Who polices them so we can move about in comparative safety? Who erects the stores, landscapes the parks, builds the freeways? Who provides the services that keep things going in good weather and bad?

---

3   Barry, Hawkins, *Francis Schaeffer and the Shape of Evangelical America* (Eerdmans, 2008).

$ettle the Discussion Questions

1. What does the Bible say about profits, rewards, and entrepreneurship?

2. Since we replicate what we celebrate, if you and I really believe that profits are good, how can we bring our full self to the table? What areas of excellence and competency can we bring to our company, industry, and team that we know we have slacked off on? How can we create an environment that honors the truth, values truthful feedback (even if it's bad news), and celebrates excellence without perfectionism? What is one way you could celebrate catching employees doing things well?

3. "What would I do if profits were good, but not everything?" I don't know the complexity of your industry, personal decisions, and financial decisions. So let me leave you with a decision and a question: How would you spend your money and make decisions if profits were good, but not everything? Would you give more money away? Would you find ways to build a business that helps the underemployed and makes less profit annually but gives jobs to those who need it (Rich Palmer investor story), etc.?

4. Whistle While You Profit by realizing Profits R Good, but Profits R Not Enough. If they are not the ultimate thing, how do we pay differently and profit differently?

5. "Does my faith affect my giving and spending at all?" "Am I giving financially in a way that really affects my lifestyle and reveals this is a priority?"

$how $upport

Search for and watch the Dave Thomas story (Wendy's) online with parent's permission.

Create a systemized way in your personal life, family life, and business to celebrate what you want to replicate. Do you want profits? At all costs? How do you create ways to celebrate those who profit, but aren't worshiping profit? How do you celebrate work and punish laziness, while revealing how each person's contribution helps the whole organization? Do you honor and celebrate stories of tremendous giving in your department? Do you teach others to work, profit, and give? When is the last time you celebrated their giving? When is the last time you modeled it yourself by letting others know how you are practicing gleaning principles and tell about the joy you have at work, why you love what you love, how it fuels the blessing in your life? Write out a plan to start celebrating what you want to see replicating.

Introduction

As we have learned through this series, God cares about the economics of business and entrepreneurship. These *Godonomics* principles allow you to whistle while you work with purpose, meaning, and a sense of being "called" to leadership. So what is leadership? That's the age-old question.

In every arena of life there are "couldas" — we coulda kept doing what we are doing. We coulda expanded. We coulda switched schools. We coulda coasted on our success. We coulda tried a new market instead of just using the same ones. We coulda held out for a better person to date, we coulda started saving more, spending less, and giving more. We coulda cut costs and streamlined despite the "rip the Band-Aid off" pain in short term. We coulda made a succession plan. We coulda ignored the dysfunction in the organization caused by the boss's son's inability to manage. There are lots of things we could do. The leader is the one that turns "couldas" into "shouldas" by engaging the minds, hearts, and hands of his followers so that the decision, while hard, or new, or different, moves from what we could do, to what we should do as an organization or family.

Read Nehemiah 4:1–23.

Nehemiah's Plan

When Sanballat heard that we were rebuilding the wall, he became angry and was greatly incensed. He ridiculed the Jews, and in the presence of his associates and the army of Samaria, he said, "What are those feeble Jews doing? Will they restore their wall? Will they offer sacrifices? Will they finish in a day? Can they bring the stones back to life from those heaps of rubble — burned as they are?"

Tobiah the Ammonite, who was at his side, said, "What they are building — even a fox climbing up on it would break down their wall of stones!"

Hear us, our God, for we are despised. Turn their insults back on their own heads. Give them over as plunder in a land of captivity. Do not cover up their guilt or blot out their sins from your sight, for they have thrown insults in the face of the builders.

So we rebuilt the wall till all of it reached half its height, for the people worked with all their heart.

But when Sanballat, Tobiah, the Arabs, the Ammonites and the people of Ashdod heard that the repairs to Jerusalem's walls had gone ahead and that the gaps were being closed, they were very angry. They all plotted together to come and fight against Jerusalem and stir up trouble against it. But we prayed to our God and posted a guard day and night to meet this threat.

Meanwhile, the people in Judah said, "The strength of the laborers is giving out, and there is so much rubble that we cannot rebuild the wall."

Also our enemies said, "Before they know it or see us, we will be right there among them and will kill them and put an end to the work."

Then the Jews who lived near them came and told us ten times over, "Wherever you turn, they will attack us."

Therefore I stationed some of the people behind the lowest points of the wall at the exposed places, posting them by families, with their swords, spears and bows. After I looked things over, I stood up and said to the nobles, the officials and the rest of the people, "Don't be afraid of them. Remember the Lord, who is great and awesome, and fight for your families, your sons and your daughters, your wives and your homes."

When our enemies heard that we were aware of their plot and that God had frustrated it, we all returned to the wall, each to our own work.

From that day on, half of my men did the work, while the other half were equipped with spears, shields, bows and armor. The officers posted themselves behind all the people of Judah who were building the wall. Those who carried materials did their work with one hand and held a weapon in the other, and each of the builders wore his sword at his side as he worked. But the man who sounded the trumpet stayed with me.

Then I said to the nobles, the officials and the rest of the people, "The work is extensive and spread out, and we are widely separated from each other along the wall. Wherever you hear the sound of the trumpet, join us there. Our God will fight for us!"

So we continued the work with half the men holding spears, from the first light of dawn till the stars came out. At that time I also said to the people, "Have every man and his helper stay inside Jerusalem at night, so they can serve us as guards by night and as workers by day." Neither I nor my brothers nor my men nor the guards with me took off our clothes; each had his weapon, even when he went for water. (NIV)

$tart the DVD $ession

(33 minutes)

1. _____ turn "couldas" to "shouldas" in the minds, hearts, and hands of followers.

2. Learning to lead on all _____ levels creates ownership and followers who fight for your values.

3. The first step is to _____ the 4. _____.

5. One of the greatest leaders in the Bible is Nehemiah. He brought a joy to leadership. And he had a challenging mission and vision. While working as the _____ to the king, he prayed, planned, and assessed what he had, what he needed, and why it was an imperative to go now.

6. Nehemiah had trust and influence with the king of Persia, but he was a foreign captive. He had no power in the organizational chart. He had to lead from the _____ of the pack through influence. That's where most of us are; we always have someone we need to convince by engaging their head as a leader. We know the naivety of those in entry-level leadership who assume power comes from position rather than influence.

7. Nehemiah engaged the mind of the king by giving the what, when, why, and _____.

8. You can start now wherever you work, whatever family you are in, in whatever position you find yourself. Lead now, and learn skills to lead from the middle of the pack, because whether you are a CEO influencing a board and stockholders or a division manager influencing an owner, we all need to do what _____ did and influence those in authority over and around us.

A tool to help engage the minds of those around you is the three C's

What: 9. _____, 10. _____, 11. _____.

The wall of Jerusalem is broken down, and its gates have been burned with fire (Nehemiah 1:3; NIV).

Where:

Then the king said to me, "What do you request?"

So I prayed to the God of heaven. . . .

Furthermore I said to the king, "If it pleases the king, let letters be given to me for the governors of the region beyond the River, that they must permit me to pass through till I come to Judah, and a letter to Asaph the keeper of the king's forest, that he must give me timber to make beams for the gates of the citadel which pertains to the temple, for the city wall, and for the house that I will occupy" (Nehemiah 2:4–8).

12. The _____ is key in moving people, especially children, but also employees because you want to mark the values into their hearts in such a way they will "own the values" and "defend the values."

13. Nehemiah has to solve a dilemma. He has extreme opposition from neighboring territories, a past record of failure, incredible odds, and a small team. Also, the work needs to balance two often contradictory values: speed and quality. The only way they can build the walls is quickly before enemies tear them down. But they are only good if they are built to a quality that will defend the walls. So Nehemiah creates an ingenious solution to the ownership issue that guarantees speed and quality. He has each man build the section of walls directly adjacent to his future residence. They will want it built quickly to have their houses protected and want quality so their homes aren't the first attacked. He has their heads with the idea "we need to build a wall in such and such days" and gave them _____ over the project. They feel the shoulda. We have to get this built and I want to do it right.

14. Sam Walton captured the _____ of his employees by giving them more ownership.

15. The other value of ownership and imparting the "why" into the heart is that employees and kids fight for the values of the company because they _____ them in their heart.

One of the roles of a leader is to 16. _____ 17. _____, which is like a paintbrush used to paint into the hearts of followers.

18. Employees who work for a _____ agree when the boss is in the room.

19. _____ want to know why because parents told them why, unlike boomers and busters.

The Curse of Knowledge

We've all worked for people with great ideas, and great speeches. We know what needs to be done and why it needs to be done, but the leader or board, or team, or pastor, or father just couldn't articulate how to do it, make it happen, or put a plan into motion. That causes frustration.

A heart and head that are ready to go, that doesn't have a plan you can put your hands to is frustrating. One of the things that makes us bad at leading and motivating as parents and presidents is what Kelleher's *Made to Stick* calls the curse of knowledge. We often know too much about our subject: medicine, the law, marketing, education, or even the Bible, so when we talk to employees or others, they get lost in an ocean of words and conflicting initiatives. We need to make our expectations clear and simple. Make them sticky.

Why: " 'Come and let us build the wall of Jerusalem, that we may no longer be a reproach.' And I told them of the hand of my God which had been good upon me, and also of the king's words that he had spoken to me. So they said, 'Let us rise up and build.' Then they set their hands to this good work" (Nehemiah 2:17–18).

20. _____ knew that when we connect, people work to a greater value of God's: a transcendent truth, it engages people in deeper ways, more purposeful ways. He showed them that this building was part of God's plan for protecting the weak, opening business opportunities for them and their neighbors, and allowing their city to be reborn according to a promise God made 70 years earlier.

Your head can get so full of the curse of knowledge that you're never able to make it 21. _____ and 22. _____ enough that people know what to do.

23. Millennials: tell them _____ what we want and the role they play.

Jesus engaged the hearts of His 24. _____, the ones killing Him, by saying, "Father 25. _____ them, for they know not what they do."

$ettle the Discussion Questions

1. As a leader, do you default to one of the three and are weak in another? Do you give others "just the facts" without capturing their hearts, or give great passionate pictures of what could be without clear plans of "how to"? Which of the three are you missing to influence? Head, heart, or hands of your followers?

Jesus did all three for us. Jesus was the ultimate example of someone who engaged the head by explaining difficult, complex theological concepts in simple phrases. He challenged the intellectuals, lawyers, and philosophers of His day to think about His message deeply. He answered the what, why, when, and how questions that people asked about faith.

Jesus went after the heart of His followers by being willing to give it all up for them. He died for them, served them, suffered for them, and lived unselfishly for them. They ended up dying for Him because He paid a debt they could never pay and offered them access to God's presence — eternal life. Jesus also inspired their hands. He told His disciples exactly what to do. He told them to love their enemies, and work diligently in a way that was attractive to supervisors who didn't believe. He told them to look for opportunities to live for others and tell others the reason for their belief. He told them to "love God with your heart and soul" and to "love your neighbor as yourself." When you wrestle with what Jesus did for you, and allow that to impact your head, heart, and hands, it provides the power and the example to do that for others. Think of it this way — in three years, Jesus, as a leader, started a movement that is still expanding and growing 2,000 years later, using no technology and only 12 leaders or disciples. Pretty impressive!

What is your obstacle to faith in God?

What is your obstacle as a leader?

Head?

Heart?

Hands?

If you begin to work on the idea you are "missing," you can grow spiritually.

If you know the area you are weak in as a leader, you can turn "couldas" into "shouldas" for your followers, too.

Introduction

Time is a precious commodity. Where does it go?

Over the course of a lifetime, the average American will spend six months sitting at stop lights, eight months opening junk mail, one year searching for misplaced items, two years trying to return phone calls, and five years waiting in line!

What does God say here about time management (work and rest)?

1. **It is something that can be learned?**

   Psalm 90:12

   So teach us to number our days, That we may gain a heart of wisdom.

2. **It is something that requires planning?**

   Ephesians 5:15–17

   See then that you walk circumspectly, not as fools but as wise, redeeming the time, because the days are evil. Therefore do not be unwise, but understand what the will of the Lord is.

Wise people plan rest and work rhythms into their lives. Look at the action words — "redeem," which means to "buy back" your time and "walk circumspectly," which means "make the most" or take advantage of. By doing this, you understand the will of God. Planning our time helps us understand God's will.

How can I make sure I am being a good steward of this gift from God, this slice of time that I call "my life"?

$tart the DVD $ession

(37 minutes)

Compose Your Own Opus

As we pursue a rhythm of rest, work, and relationships, we will need to compose our own opus.

The rhythms of life are much more like a piece of music than they are a machine. There are highs, lows, loud, soft, moments of rest, and moments of notes. Each of us has a unique one — a unique opus that plays to our strengths, our best times to grow, our best times to produce, and rest.

Composing your own opus for the rhythm of your life is critical to learning how to whistle while you work, play, and rest.

As we look at composing our own original opus, we need to examine three times in our life: prime time, grime time, and unwind time.

Everyone can Whistle While They Work by examining three times: *prime time, grime time, and unwind time.*

We'll work better and in a more sustainable way if we create a rhythm to three times.

The first time is our "prime time."

I. Be Aware of Your Prime Time.

We need to 1. _____ these three "times" to make sure we're managing a 2. _____ or an opus that allows them all to play notes on the page. TV shows know there are "prime times" when people sit down after all the busyness to watch. It's where they put the best shows, the best advertisements, etc.

3. You and I have a prime time as well. Some of us have prime times in the morning, some in the evening, some of us have bursts of leadership and creativity when we "get away" for two or three days. You and I have to learn how to compose the _____ opus of our prime time.

    Paul mentions this idea in a short passage in Ephesisans 5:15–17: "See then that you walk circumspectly, not as fools but as wise, redeeming the time, because the days are evil. Therefore do not be unwise, but understand what the will of the Lord is."

4. Prioritizing our prime time begins as we stop walking foolishly by wisely examining our time and rest. When we begin to walk wisely, we _____ the time by walking circumspectly. Walking circumspectly means to "notice in advance," and "see dangers before they occur" and watch out where you put your feet.

Prime time is about injecting 5. _____ into your 6. _____. Time is limited, but not as limited as your energy.

So what is your prime time? How can you "walk circumspectly"?

7. Let's add a suggestion for "walking wisely" with your time. Figure out where your prime time is daily and add _____ minutes a day to your prime time — that equals 182.5 hours of greater productivity each year.

8. People do their _____ thinking, creating, and innovating in their prime time. Ironically, you may want to avoid using your prime time for your highest priorities because what you

love comes easily. Use your prime time for lower, medium, or multitasking priorities, rather than doing what only you can do. When you keep your best work in your best time slot, your productivity and energy goes way up. So know your prime time, but also know your wasted time. Then there are other times that are "grime time" where you grind through work, but it's not the most "sweet spot" type of work. It's the lower, medium, less "in your zone" work.

Ephesians 5:15 "Redeem the time"

II. Examine Your Grime Time

The grime time is that "get your hands dirty" and get to it time of day — the rhythm of your day whereby you crank through multiple projects or to-dos at once.

The Bible offers wisdom on how to 9. _____ your prime time, but also how to 10. _____ 11. _____ your grime time.

12. Paul uses the phrase "redeeming the time," which means to maximize the time, or "buy back" time that is lost or could be lost. Our _____ time is that time in our day that is not our ideal creative, productive, best time, but the "get 'er done" grind-through-the-details time that we all need to do weekly. In order to maximize our time, we need to look at our grime time in a few ways.

In order to use our grind time well, we will need to maximize our opportunities (v. 16).

Convert Minutes into Moments

The Bible is written in Greek and has two words for time 13. _____ and 14, _____.

Transform your chronos, 15. _____, into kairos, 16. _____.

We all say, "I could get more done if I had more *chronos*" (more days and hours), but that is a waste of time. We all say we want more time, but you never get more time. There is no more *chronos* for any of us.

17. You never, ever get more time, so instead we convert *chronos* into *kairos* by turning minutes into _____.

Kairos moments occur all the time. They occur when there are moments within the day, the hour, and the week. It's a recognition that "this is important," "this is a moment," or "this should be a moment or opportunity to redeem."

The word "redeem" means to, 18. _____ 19. _____. We must do something here. We must see life a certain way. We must view the moment in a day.

This is how we transform "grime time" into "meaningful time":

- I need to make this car ride a time to connect with my teens, not take up a business call.

- I need to use this season of my marriage to its fullest by planning date nights.

- I need to see my relationships in my community and business as potential ways God will use me to share His story.

- I need to see patterns into the future, and make decisions now to prepare for the worst.

- I must capture my daughter's heart now (whether she is 3, 13, or 30).

- I must instruct and overlap my schedule with my kids to be an influencer now. I must reject the lie that "I'm too busy," which is another flavor of "sooner or later," and shake myself into reality by saying, "This is not a priority, but it should be!"

There are three quick applications on how to maximize our grime time while protecting our prime time.

1) Maximize Our Prime Time — High-Priority Items

Putting 20. _____ 21. _____ in our prime time makes us more effective.

2) Maximize Our Grind Time — Medium-to Low-Priority Items

Putting 22. _____ and 23. _____ priorities in our grime time makes us more effective.

3). Maximize Our Unwind Time — Increase Inputs to Maximize Output

Ephesians 5 says, "Do not be unwise, but understand what the will of the Lord is."

24. We can often find ourselves "chopping wood" week in and week out without _____ our unwind time.

25. We need the unwind time to bring out the beauty. God's will and plan for our life comes out when we are _____ enough to use our unwind time and rest and refuel.

Ephesians 5:17

Therefore do not be unwise, but understand what the will of the Lord is.

26. God's _____ is a rhythm of rest, productivity, creativity, and relationship.

27. His will is not to turn us into productive machines of output, but to help us find the music that allows us to flourish. Do I have quiet times, loud times, times of rest? Those are the _____ that make music out of our lives. If God wanted to speak to me, if I wanted to reflect on what I am enjoying or disappointed about in my life, is there any time to reflect and refuel, and rest in the rhythm of my life?

Working in It — Not on It

We are often so busy working 28. _____ that we don't work 29. _____. We are so busy running our department and keeping our jobs and heads above water, we don't have or make the time to step back, slow down and work on it.

30. Unwind time includes rest, fun, and contemplation of "working on it" — this is time spent with God, others, or ourselves. We need to _____ mentally because we're still holding grudges, and we can't be _____.

$ettle the Discussion Questions

1. Are you aware of your prime time? What is the best time of day to do your best, creative, "in the zone" work? Do you schedule your best work to be done during your prime time slots? Are you "walking" wisely in the use of your time? Explain:

2. In his book *Extreme Productivity*, Robert C. Pozen, who writes for *Harvard Business Review*, notes that we need to write down our top priority goals and then look at our schedule and see if even 50 percent of our time goes to the top priorities.[1] Write down your top priority goals. Does your schedule reflect even 50 percent? How can you improve your time management?

---

1   Robert C. Pozen, *Extreme Productivity*, (New York: HarperCollins, 2012).

3. Consider what is was like to listen to a piece of Mozart's *Opus*, with and without rests. What emotions came out as it was played without any rests? It felt frantic, rushed, without rhythm. That's how many of us are running our lives — with no rests. We are not enjoying the music of our lives the way it is made. Our opus is squashed by our speed and lack of rests and moments of slowing down.

When the piece was played with rests, did you hear the difference? Did you feel the difference? The music was better with rests. It needs the unwind time to bring out the beauty. God's will and plan for our life comes out when we are wise enough to use our unwind time to rest and refuel. How does the difference between the two versions impact how you see rest as part of your life?

4. A Kayan woodcutter asked for a job with a timber merchant. He got the job with a good salary and decent work conditions. And so, the woodcutter was determined to do his best for the boss. His boss gave him an axe and on his first day, the woodcutter cut down 15 trees. The boss was pleased and said, "Well done, good work!" Highly motivated, the woodcutter tried harder the next day, but he only could bring down 13 trees. The third day, he tried even harder, but he was only able to bring down 11 trees. Day after day, he tried harder but cut down a fewer number of trees. *I must be losing my strength*, the Kayan man thought. He apologized to the boss, claiming he could not understand why. "When was the last time you sharpened your axe?" the boss asked. "Sharpen? I had no time to sharpen my axe. I have been too busy cutting down trees." He sharpened his axe and immediately was back to 15 trees a day. Since that conversation, he begins the day by sharpening his axe. What have you learned from this story and how does it apply to your life?

5. How can you simplify your life? Do you really need all those "things" that fill your life? Things that obligate you to give your time to low-priority things that could be better spent focused on high-priority things? Write a list of your obligations that should be simplified or removed in order to focus on higher-priority things. Be sure to evaluate:

    A. Physical clutter — things that occupy my space that do not need to.

    B. Mental clutter — things that occupy my mind that do not need to. Do I spend time listening, watching, reading things that are "time wasters"? Do I need to listen, watch, and reflect on music, reading, and thoughts that will help me unwind?

    C. Emotional clutter — things that occupy my heart that do not need to.

        Are there hurts you need to let go of, people you need to forgive, forgiveness you need to ask for, relationships you need to restore?

6. As we compose our own opus, we need to look at our prime time, our grime time, and our unwind time and look at rhythms that allow us to refuel and give our best times to our best practices. We need to purposely refuel our creative leadership tanks with intentional inefficient unwind time. Which of the times are you good at, and which are you bad at? Begin to compose your own opus. Write it down in detail.

7. "This revolutionary organization will be positioned to dramatically outperform its peers. In our latest meta-analysis the Gallup Organization asked this question of 198,000 employees working in 7,939 business units within 36 companies: At work do you have the opportunity to do what you do best every day? We then compared the responses to the performance of the business units and discovered the following: When employees answered strongly agree to this question, they were 50 percent more likely to work in business units with lower employee turnover, 38 percent more likely to work in more productive business units, and 44 percent more likely to work in business units with higher customer satisfaction scores. And over time those business units that increased the number of employees who strongly agreed saw comparable increases in productivity, customer loyalty, and employee retention. Whichever way you care to slice the data, the organization whose employees feel that their strengths are used every day is more powerful and more robust.

    This is very good news for the organization that wants to be on the vanguard of the strengths revolution. Why? Because most organizations remain startlingly inefficient at capitalizing on the strengths of their people. In Gallup's total database we have asked the 'opportunity to do what I do best' question of more than 1.7 million employees in 101 companies from 63 countries. What percentage do you think strongly agrees that they have an opportunity to do what they do best every day? What percentage truly feels that their strengths are in play?

    Twenty percent. Globally, only 20 percent of employees working in the large organizations we surveyed feel that their strengths are in play every day. Most bizarre of all, the longer an employee stays with an organization and the higher he climbs the traditional career ladder, the less likely he is to strongly agree that he is playing to his strengths."[2]

How does this statement affect how you will evaluate a prospective position with a company? How does it affect your views of employment and your role within a company?

---

2   Marcus Buckingham and Donald O. Clifton, *Now, Discover Your Strengths* (New York: Free Press, 2001); http://businessjour-nal.gallup.com/content/547/strengths-revolution.aspx

$tudy the $ummary $tatements

There is probably one area of time you do better than others. Some of us are laser-focused and know what we do well and make that "the priority" of our lives, and calendars, but we won't unwind well. We need to get out a calendar and once a month schedule a chance to "work on it" by unwinding with recreation, a counselor for our marriage to work on it, an off-site before there's an emergency, or a fun day to refresh. Others of us have allowed grime time to bleed out all our prime time. What percentage of your week is spent on what you do best and can most uniquely do to advance the work of your organization? When in your weekly, monthly, and yearly schedules will you work on your prime time priorities? Do you know your strengths? How will you work with your board, boss, family, team, or teacher to increase more time into your strengths?

$how $upport

Read the following from the *Harvard Business Review*:

Steve Wanner is a highly respected 37-year-old partner at Ernst & Young, married with four young children. When we met him a year ago, he was working 12 to 14 hour days, felt perpetually exhausted, and found it difficult to fully engage with his family in the evenings, which left him feeling guilty and dissatisfied. He slept poorly, made no time to exercise, and seldom ate healthy meals, instead grabbing a bite to eat on the run or while working at his desk.

Wanner's experience is not uncommon. Most of us respond to rising demands in the workplace by putting in longer hours, which inevitably take a toll on us physically, mentally, and emotionally. That leads to declining levels of engagement, increasing levels of distraction, high turnover rates, and soaring medical costs among employees. We at the Energy Project have worked with thousands of leaders and managers in the course of doing consulting and coaching at large organizations during the past five years. With remarkable consistency, these executives tell us they're pushing themselves harder than ever to keep up and increasingly feel they are at a breaking point.

The core problem with working longer hours is that time is a finite resource. Energy is a different story. Defined in physics as the capacity to work, energy comes from four main wellsprings in human beings: the body, emotions, mind, and spirit. In each, energy can be systematically expanded and regularly renewed by establishing specific rituals — behaviors that are intentionally practiced and precisely scheduled, with the goal of making them unconscious and automatic as quickly as possible.

To effectively reenergize their workforces, organizations need to shift their emphasis from getting more out of people to investing more in them, so they are motivated — and able — to bring more of themselves to work every day. To recharge themselves, individuals need to recognize the costs of energy-depleting behaviors and then take responsibility for changing them, regardless of the circumstances they're facing.[1]

1　Tony Schwartz and Catherine McCarthy, "Manage Your Energy, Not Your Time," *Harvard Business Review*, October 2007, http://hbr.org/2007/10/manage-your-energy-not-your-time.

Write a Report

Write a report outlining the steps Steve Wanner could take to manage his time more effectively. Also, explain how his company could encourage employees to manage their time more effectively in order to get the best out of their work. Give practical ideas.

Introduction

We all love being near generous people. Generosity increases curiosity. Generosity decreases animosity as people sense a genuine desire to give, love, and bless.

When many people think of God, they think of a judge or perhaps a big marshmallow ball of love. Others assume God is serious, stoic, "appropriate," or sterile. Some see God as stingy, doling out limited resources to the most hard-working, and only having so much forgiveness for small mistakes or one-time infractions. This is a God you respect. A God you fear. A God you keep your distance from because being called to see your Heavenly Father is like being called to the principal's office.

There is a picture of the transcendence of God taught in the Bible. God is the law, the judge, the enforcer. Yet, God is also imminent. He is the neighbor, the friend who is up close and personal. That's the God of the Bible, a perfect mix of perfection; but what many don't realize is that what God is known for is HIS generosity — of love, grace, forgiveness, and mercy. Generosity increases curiosity toward God as we long to get to know Him. Generosity decreases animosity as our fear fades away.

$tart the DVD $ession

(35 minutes)

1. Generosity increases _____.

2. Generosity decreases _____.

3. Explore three areas where God gives: the garden, the tabernacle, and the Church through His _____.

God Gives in the Garden

Genesis 1:1

In the beginning God created the heavens and the earth.

The first verse of the Bible struggles to communicate the full character of the God it is introducing as the grammar is already in conflict. God — singular, plural. The Bible begins by introducing us to a generous, other-centered, triune God who is filled with joy and giving. He is three parts in one, and each person loves to give to the other. They adapt to each other in relationship, look out for each other, enjoy each other, ask each other what each person would prefer, and they try to outgive each other. In the dance of the Trinity, the greatest is the one who is most self-effacing, most sacrificial, most devoted to the good of the other. And this generous God can't keep His joy, peace, and life to Himself; He makes mankind to spread the community, love, and creativity with the world. So in an explosion of creativity and generous giving, He makes the world.

Genesis 1:2

And the Spirit of God was hovering over the face of the waters.

The Bible says that the spirit of the Lord hovered or danced above the waters, preparing to speak seven times with generous creative power over the world. He gives light, moons, stars; He gives flowers and creeping things; He gives of himself with colors, vegetation, light, and darkness.

Then He turns to His crowning achievement as He makes men and women by saying, "Let us make man in our image." What image? We are made in three parts in one — like God. We have a body, soul, and spirit. We long for community. We hunger for giving of ourselves through work, relationships, and creative interaction with our world, but God was also creating engines of generosity in the world as well.

> Then God said, "Let Us make man in Our image, according to Our likeness; let them have dominion over the fish of the sea, over the birds of the air, and over the cattle, over all the earth and over every creeping thing that creeps on the earth." So God created man in His own image; in the image of God He created him; male and female He created them. . . . And the LORD God formed man of the dust of the ground, and breathed into his nostrils the breath of life; and man became a living being (Genesis. 1:26–2:7).

Worldview Note: Pantheists usually believe that God, so to speak, animates the universe as you animate your body: that the universe almost is God, so that if it did not exist He would not exist either, and anything you find in the universe is a part of God. The Christian idea is quite different. They think God invented and made the universe — like a man making a picture or composing a tune. A painter is not a picture, and he does not die if his picture is destroyed. You may say, "He's put a lot of himself into it," but you only mean that all its beauty and interest has come out of his head. His skill is not in the picture in the same way that it is in his head, or even in his hands. See how this difference between pantheists and Christians hangs together with the other one? If you do not take the distinction between good and bad very seriously, then it is easy to say that anything you find in this world is a part of God. But, of course, if you think some things are really bad, and God really good, then you cannot talk like that.

4. In the Garden, we are introduced to a God who _____.

Many cultures had stories that depicted the beginning of the world and human history as the result of a struggle between warring cosmic forces. In the Babylonian creation story the *Enuma Elish*, the god Marduk overcomes the goddess Tiamat and forges the world out of her remains. In this and similar accounts, the visible universe was an uneasy balance of powers in tension with one another.

In the Bible, however, creation is not the result of a conflict, for God has no rivals. Indeed, all the powers and beings of heaven and earth are created by Him and dependent on Him.

Just like God, we are designed for 5. _____, 6. _____, and 7. _____.

The Greeks' account of creation includes the idea of successive "ages of mankind," beginning with a golden age. During this age, human beings and gods lived on the earth together in harmony. This sounds at first vaguely like the story of the Garden of Eden, but one dissimilarity is very telling. The poet Hesiod tells us that the "earth simply provided food in abundance."

The Book of Genesis could not have been more different. Repeatedly the first chapters of the Book of Genesis describes God who 8. _____, using the Hebrew *mlkh*, the word for ordinary 9. _____ 10. _____. As one scholar put it, it is wholly "unexpected that the extraordinary divine activity involved in creating heaven and earth should be so described."[1]

11. In the beginning, then, *God worked*. Work was not a necessary _____ that came into the picture later, or something human beings were created to do but that was beneath the great God Himself. No, God worked for the sheer joy of it. Work could not have a more exalted inauguration.

1   Timothy Keller, *The Insider and the Outcast* (New York: Penguin, 2013).

God gives in the garden, then he gives in the tabernacle, too.

When God led people out of Egypt, He wanted them to be a people of liberty, productivity, and generosity. He wanted to teach them how to be a free and 12. _____ people.

The major difference between free enterprise and communism, socialism, and Marxism is two words: 13. _____ 14. _____

15. Governor Bradford saw this firsthand at America's founding. He first tried _____, or communal living. After two years of everyone "working" for the common good, half the population died and the model had completely failed. After all, if a community of devout religious people couldn't make it work, what hope was there for it ever being successful?

Bradford went back to the 16. _____ and saw God's law and 17. _____ 18. _____ principles. He tried to apply three principles from God to his society: property rights, incentive, and personal freedom.

19. After a season of implementing the new model using God's principles, something amazing happened. Family members who were "too tired" or "too sick" to work suddenly came alive. Husbands and wives, children and cousins worked together on their own farms. Each person and family had _____ to work hard and provide for themselves and those they cared about most. The result was a bumper crop. There was so much bounty and so much provision that they had plenty for themselves and others. Thus, they celebrated the first Thanksgiving to thank God for His provision and His wisdom, which made a town's economy work.

20. God laid these principles in place because He wanted people to have property so they could _____ it and give it away.

Here's what's amazing: God will spend 25 chapters outlining the details for a place to meet and know and experience His generous gift of forgiveness. While the Tabernacle had 25 chapters of the Bible devoted to it, creation itself was only given two chapters of explanation. Why?

Creation	Tabernacle
God said: I'll make it, you fill it.	Now you make it, I'll fill it.
Seven times God spoke.	Seven times God spoke.

Menorah

21. In the Holy of Holies was a Passover lamp — a menorah with seven candlesticks to remind the people of a fire; a bush, a reminder of God's _____ and hearing of their prayers and deliverance from Egypt.

22. The seven also pointed to seven feasts, or _____ God commanded His people to have. They were feasts of celebration. Giant parties with dancing, reflection, and eating together to celebrate God's generous deliverance. Many of these, like the feast of Pentecost and Unleavened Bread were at harvest time to thank God for generous provision for their food. First fruits was a time of being generous to God with the first part of your harvest to remind God of your dependence on His generosity for life. And when the tabernacle was built, the fire of God came out of the tabernacle and consumed the sacrifice as a reminder that God made a way to come close to this generous, but just God.

Incense Altar

The incense altar had a constant 23. _____ of 24. _____ to remind the people of God's guidance. The significance of the tabernacle is that it was the place God dwelled. It was a holy place, where you prayed, had feasts, got direction, and found forgiveness.

25. **Generosity Increases _____.**

26. God created a _____ for the tabernacle to increase curiosity.

27. **God Gives through the _____.**

28. At Pentecost, after Christ had given His life at the Cross and fully emptied Himself as God, fire came out and consumed the sacrifice and fire rested on the disciples. They were now the representative of God's generosity to the world, filled with purpose, joy, and comfort, and filled with His Spirit. They then went out and passed it on to _____.

1 Corinthians 6:19–20

Or do you not know that your body is the temple of the Holy Spirit who is in you, whom you have from God, and you are not your own? For you were bought at a price; therefore glorify God in your body and in your spirit, which are God's.

Emperor Julian the Apostate found that generosity increased curiosity. At one point, Julian complained about the Christians (aka "Galileans.") Read his complaint:

Why do we not observe that it is their [the Christians'] benevolence to strangers, their care for the graves of the dead and the pretended holiness of their lives that have done most to increase atheism [unbelief of the pagan gods]? . . . For it is disgraceful that, when no Jew ever has to beg, and the impious Galileans [Christians] support not only their own poor but ours as well, all men see that our people lack aid from us. Teach those of the Hellenic faith to contribute to public service of this sort."

— Julian[2]

The Bible uses the word 29. _____ for 30. _____.

2   http://www.tertullian.org/fathers/julian_apostate_letters_1_trans.htm

$ettle the Discussion Questions

1. While the Tabernacle had 25 chapters of the Bible devoted to it, creation itself was only given 2 chapters of explanation. Why?

2. What about you? Do you know a generous God who made you, leads you, made a way to forgive you, and came to earth to be generous by giving up His body for you? If so, He then sent or gave His spirit to dwell in you, to set a fire within you to change the world by spreading or sharing His love, giving, and generosity with others. It may be a percentage, God's priorities, or progressive giving. It might be caring for the poor, pregnant girls, the elderly, hurting, etc., but you can't keep it to yourself. You tell others, live for God, and help others like He's helped you. You use your talents to benefit others, not build your own kingdom, because He chose you, adopted you, and gave to you. List ways you plan to be or have been generous.

$tudy the $ummary $tatements

- Be generous with your money
- Be generous with your time
- Be generous with forgiveness
- Be generous with your body, in marriage
- Be generous with patience, longsuffering

The benefits of generosity: increased joy, part of helping others have curiosity about God, lower the animosity toward faith.

We must exhort all Christians to gain all they can and to save all they can; that is, in effect to grow rich… (and) likewise "give all they can"!

— John Wesley*

Introduction

Proverbs 31 is the basis for the title for this series. Solomon's advice covers wisdom for life that was uncommon sense for a whole generation. *Godonomics* is really God's common sense wisdom for life finances and faith. In this Proverb, we are given wisdom for life whether "from" King Lemuel or "for" King Lemuel, depending on how the Hebrew reads. Either way, it is a challenge to a leader, an influencer, or a worker, on how to work wiser.

Proverbs 31:1

The words of King Lemuel. . . .

There are a few ideas on this. One is that this is another name for Solomon (I'll talk about that more in a moment). Another view is that Lemuel was the king of Massa, which many scholars believe. Massa was one of the descendants of Ishmael and the leader of one of the Ishmaelite clans (Genesis 25:14). The name of Lemuel in Proverbs 31:1 is to identify him as the king of Massa. Wisdom literature was widely known in the Ancient Near East and Israel did not develop its wisdom tradition in a cultural vacuum. It is evident that Israel borrowed some of its wisdom traditions from neighboring countries. One good example is the inclusion of Egyptian proverbs found in the "Instructions of Amen-em-Opet" into Proverbs 22:17–24:34. Whichever, this passage is a series of wise words from a mother to a son.

Proverbs 31:1–2

. . . the utterance which his mother taught him: What, my son? And what, son of my womb? And what, son of my vows?

This chapter is a series of "wise sayings" from his mother — wisdom from a mom to a son about how to succeed in life. This mother reminds herself and her son that he is the result of a vow to God while he was in the womb, like Hannah did with Samuel, or Samson's mother. And this mother is challenging her son, "What of my vows? You are not living the life God called for you, that I prayed for you."

*www.imarc.cc/one_meth/vol-02-no-02.html

Review Proverbs 31

The words of King Lemuel, the utterance which his mother taught him:

What, my son?

And what, son of my womb?

And what, son of my vows?

Do not give your strength to women,

Nor your ways to that which destroys kings.

It is not for kings, O Lemuel,

It is not for kings to drink wine,

Nor for princes intoxicating drink;

Lest they drink and forget the law,

And pervert the justice of all the afflicted.

Give strong drink to him who is perishing,

And wine to those who are bitter of heart.

Let him drink and forget his poverty,

And remember his misery no more.

Open your mouth for the speechless,

In the cause of all who are appointed to die,

Open your mouth, judge righteously,

And plead the cause of the poor and needy.

Who can find a virtuous wife?

For her worth is far above rubies.

The heart of her husband safely trusts her;

So he will have no lack of gain.

She does him good and not evil

All the days of her life.

She seeks wool and flax,

And willingly works with her hands.

She is like the merchant ships,

She brings her food from afar.

She also rises while it is yet night,

And provides food for her household,

And a portion for her maidservants.

She considers a field and buys it;

From her profits she plants a vineyard.

She girds herself with strength,

And strengthens her arms.

She perceives that her merchandise is good,

And her lamp does not go out by night.

She stretches out her hands to the distaff,

And her hand holds the spindle.

She extends her hand to the poor,

Yes, she reaches out her hands to the needy.

She is not afraid of snow for her household,

For all her household is clothed with scarlet.

She makes tapestry for herself;

Her clothing is fine linen and purple.

Her husband is known in the gates,

When he sits among the elders of the land.

She makes linen garments and sells them,

And supplies sashes for the merchants.

Strength and honor are her clothing;

She shall rejoice in time to come.

She opens her mouth with wisdom,

And on her tongue is the law of kindness.

She watches over the ways of her household,

And does not eat the bread of idleness.

Her children rise up and call her blessed;

Her husband also, and he praises her:

"Many daughters have done well,

But you excel them all."

Charm is deceitful and beauty is passing,

But a woman who fears the LORD, she shall be praised.

Give her of the fruit of her hands,

And let her own works praise her in the gates.

$tart the DVD $ession

(31 minutes)

What Weakens Work

There are two temptations that weaken work: The tendencies to 1. _____ and 2. _____.

1. **The Temptation to Isolate**

Proverbs 31:3–7

Do not give your strength to women, nor your ways to that which destroys kings. It is not for kings, O Lemuel, it is not for kings to drink wine, nor for princes intoxicating drink; lest they drink and forget the law, and pervert the justice of all the afflicted. Give strong drink to him who is perishing, and wine to those who are bitter of heart. Let him drink and forget his poverty. . . .

3. Anyone who leads, especially a king-type leader, knows the pressure, the loneliness, and the isolation that can come from responsibility, caring for so many lives, and having your decisions impact such a large net of people. And in the midst of that pressure, there is temptation to drink away the pressure. The writer's mother warns him that this weakens work. Falling into the temptation of "women" which is "that which destroys kings." And then she mentions how "alcoholism destroys kings" and their work, and their legacies. Why? When they drink, they forget the _____ and end up perverting justice. They aren't thinking straight. They end up having clouded memory and judgment and others are hurt.

4. _____ was another name for Solomon. The Ancient Rabbis identified Lemuel with Solomon, and relate that when, on the day of the dedication of the temple, he married Pharaoh's daughter, he drank too much at the wedding feast, and slept until the fourth hour of the next day, with the keys of the temple under his pillow. Whereupon his mother, Bathsheba, entered and reproved him with this oracle. Bathsheba's own amour with Solomon's father does not appear to have excited any rabbinical suspicion that the description of the virtuous wife with which the Book of Proverbs closes is hardly characteristic of the woman.

5. In fact, this idea of "_____" is key to the passage because the writer expounds upon it in verses 7–9. While the pressures of work can tempt you to isolate yourself through alcoholism and escapism, there is another danger in that you could end up passive and not only isolated, but insulated.

2. **The Temptation to Insulate**

Proverbs 31:7–9

. . . And remember his misery no more. Open your mouth for the speechless, in the cause of all who are appointed to die. Open your mouth, judge righteously, and plead the cause of the poor and needy.

6. Twice in this passage, his mother challenges him to "open your mouth." Open your mouth for the speechless and those appointed to die and for those in the court of law, to plead the case of the _____ and needy.

The role of government or the king according to the Bible, is to enforce the 7. _____ of 8. _____.

In the Bible, the king was to make sure that the poor and needy had access to 9. _____ 10. _____.

This is not the current use of the term "social justice" today. Today, social justice is a term to talk about economic equality, which encourages government taking from one group to give to another, violating 11. _____ 12. _____.

13. So King Lemuel's mom tells him to avoid two things that _____ work: the tendencies to isolate and insulate. But what strengthens work?

What Strengthens Work

1. **A Supportive Spouse**

   Proverbs 31:10–12

   Who can find a virtuous wife? For her worth is far above rubies. The heart of her husband safely trusts her; so he will have no lack of gain. She does him good and not evil all the days of her life.

14. The wife of noble character (*hayil*) is also mentioned in Proverbs 12:4 and 31:29. Ruth was called "a woman of _____ character" (Ruth 3:11). The word for noble character is translated "capable" in Exodus 18:21.

15. Part of what strengthens work is having a _____ spouse.

16. A supportive man or woman in marriage results in both of you not "_____ gain" because you have a trusting relationship.

17. It is interesting to note that his supportive spouse is also an entrepreneur, bussinesswoman, purchaser, and _____.

2. **A Willing Work Ethic**

   Proverbs 31:13–15

   She seeks wool and flax, and willingly works with her hands. She is like the merchant ships, she brings her food from afar. She also rises while it is yet night, and provides food for her household, and a portion for her maidservants.

The phrase "willingly works" means "with the delight of her hands." This woman loves work. How and why? She sees herself as a 18. _____ 19. _____ to show people creativity, excellence, and justice.

20. As Christians, we are similar; we are ships showing _____ kingdom to an earthly kingdom by the way we work.

21. She also sees work as a way to _____ for her family and her employees. When we work smarter, we remember that every day is a chance to bless our families and our employees by fully and completely engaging in work.

22. She sees herself as God's merchant ship of everyday _____.

23. Martin Luther expounded this very thing. Martin Luther proposed this very idea of a Christian view of work when he said, "God doesn't have to do it that way but He is. He's _____ you through other people's work. And he's loving others through your work." He goes as far as to say that the baker and the farmer in work is God in disguise.

3. A Love of Profiting & Giving
Proverbs 31:16–20

She considers a field and buys it; from her profits she plants a vineyard. She girds herself with strength, and strengthens her arms. She perceives that her merchandise is good, and her lamp does not go out by night. She stretches out her hands to the distaff, and her hand holds the spindle. She extends her hand to the poor, yes, she reaches out her hands to the needy.

24. The Bible celebrates _____.

25. She uses the act of _____ as a way of blessing her customers.

26. Her love for the _____ is twice mentioned. She sees work and profit as a way to help the hurting and poor around her.

4. A Love of Spending
Proverbs 31:21–24

She is not afraid of snow for her household, for all her household is clothed with scarlet. She makes tapestry for herself; her clothing is fine linen and purple. Her husband is known in the gates, when he sits among the elders of the land. She makes linen garments and sells them, and supplies sashes for the merchants.

This woman is a fine arts dealer of high-end clothing. Scarlet, purple, fine linen. Garments for the leaders in the land. Sashes and supplies for merchants. This woman knows how to buy, supply, and make high-end clothing. In fact, she sat in the city gates, the commerce center where the elders sat and would make and sell high-end garments for customers.

27. The _____ esteems this businesswoman as a purchasing agent, a manufacturer, with an eye to beauty, aesthetics, and design.

28. She is honoring _____ with her eye for fashion and beauty and smart purchases.

5. A Love of God through Work

Proverbs 31:27–31

She watches over the ways of her household, and does not eat the bread of idleness. . . . But a woman who fears the LORD, she shall be praised. Give her of the fruit of her hands, and let her own works praise her in the gates.

29. Now, what fuels *Godonomics* and allows you to "whistle while you work" and have "common sense" in your work is a fear of the _____. This is what strengthens work. Yes, it's a supportive spouse, a love of profit and giving, and spending, but loving God and others through your work is critical, and totally counter-cultural.

Worldview Note:

The Greeks understood that life in the world required work, but they believed that not all work was created equal. Work that used the mind rather than the body was nobler, less beastly. The highest form of work was the most cognitive and the least manual. The whole Greek social structure helped to support such an outlook, for it rested on the premise that slaves and craftsmen did the work, enabling the elite to devote themselves to the exercise of the mind in art, philosophy, and politics.

Aristotle very famously said in his *Politics I.V.8* that some people are born to be slaves. He meant that some people are not as capable of higher rational thought and therefore should do the work that frees the more talented and brilliant to pursue a life of honor and culture. Modern people bristle with outrage at such a statement, but while we do not today hold with the idea of literal slavery, the attitudes behind Aristotle's statement are alive and well. Christian philosopher Lee Hardy and many others have argued that this Greek attitude toward work and its place in human life was largely preserved in both the thought and "practice of the Christian church" through the centuries, and still holds a great deal of influence today in our culture.

What has come down to us is a set of pervasive ideas. One is that work is a necessary evil. The only good work, in this view, is work that helps us make money so that we can support our families and pay others to do menial work. Second, we believe that lower-status or lower-paying work is an assault on our dignity. One result of this belief is that many people take jobs that they are not suited for at all, choosing to aim for careers that do not fit their gifts but promise higher wages and prestige.

Western societies are increasingly divided between the highly remunerated "knowledge classes" and the more poorly remunerated "service sector," and most of us accept and perpetuate the value judgments that attach to these categories. Another result is that many people will choose to be unemployed rather than do work that they feel is beneath them, and most service and manual labor falls into this category.

$ettle the Discussion Questions

1. As you head off into the world of work, what advice do you think your mother would write to you in a letter? What advice given to Lemuel will you make a point to remember? What advice would you give to your son or daughter as they take they their place in the workplace?

2. Proverbs 31 outlines a woman of honor that profits her family. What things should you look for in a spouse?

3. Consider the Greek worldview of work. How do you see this attitude reflected in society today? How is this in contrast to the teachings found in the Bible?

$tudy the $ummary $tatements

In summary, let's go back to one image given to us — the merchant ship in verse 14: She is like the merchant ships, she brings her food from afar.

For the next seven days, think about your work as a merchant ship. God has called you to sail a merchant ship from one "far-off land" to another. We are representatives of another land: God's land, God's Kingdom. Through our work, we deliver cargo to this world. We deliver His love, His justice, His compassion, His mercy, His creativity, and His culture through our work.

Wherever you go on Monday . . . sail the ship. You are His merchant ship. Because you are his merchant ship bringing needed goods from one kingdom to another, do not weaken your work by isolation or insulation. But instead sail the merchant ship by revealing a love of work, profit, giving, spending, and God that flows through the Monday–Friday Seas.

God will love others through your work when you sail well.

Introduction

As we read through Proverbs, it's helpful to have an understanding of Hebrew poetry. So let's look at two concepts of Hebrew poetry that are used in Proverbs 13.

Parallelism and Personification

Hebrew poetry rhymes ideas rather than sounds most of the time. That's helpful — since we are reading it in English, we can "catch" a lot of the poetry despite the translation into English.

The Proverbs often introduce us to memorable characters that have a sticky factor to help "glue lessons" to us. Wisdom and foolishness become "persons" through personification. The Bible introduces us to these characters of wisdom and foolishness as people so we can remember what to imitate and what to avoid. These common sense principles show us how *Godonomics* work in our living and spending.

Read Proverbs 13

A wise son *heeds* his father's instruction,

But a scoffer does not listen to rebuke.

A man shall eat well by the fruit of *his* mouth,

But the soul of the unfaithful feeds on violence.

He who guards his mouth preserves his life,

But he who opens wide his lips shall have destruction.

The soul of a lazy man desires, and has nothing;

But the soul of the diligent shall be made rich.

A righteous man hates lying,

But a wicked man is loathsome and comes to shame.

Righteousness guards *him* whose way is blameless,

But wickedness overthrows the sinner.

There is one who makes himself rich, yet has nothing;

And one who makes himself poor, yet has great riches.

The ransom of a man's life is his riches,

But the poor does not hear rebuke.

The light of the righteous rejoices,

But the lamp of the wicked will be put out.

By pride comes nothing but strife,

But with the well-advised is wisdom.

Wealth gained by dishonesty will be diminished,

But he who gathers by labor will increase.

Hope deferred makes the heart sick,

But when the desire comes, it is a tree of life.

He who despises the word will be destroyed,

But he who fears the commandment will be rewarded.

The law of the wise is a fountain of life,

To turn one away from the snares of death.

Good understanding gains favor,

But the way of the unfaithful is hard.

Every prudent man acts with knowledge,

But a fool lays open his folly.

A wicked messenger falls into trouble,

But a faithful ambassador brings health.

Poverty and shame will come to him who disdains correction,

But he who regards a rebuke will be honored.

A desire accomplished is sweet to the soul,

But it is an abomination to fools to depart from evil.

He who walks with wise men will be wise,

But the companion of fools will be destroyed.

Evil pursues sinners,

But to the righteous, good shall be repaid.

A good man leaves an inheritance to his children's children,

But the wealth of the sinner is stored up for the righteous.

Much food is in the fallow ground of the poor,

And for lack of justice there is waste.

He who spares his rod hates his son,

But he who loves him disciplines him promptly.

The righteous eats to the satisfying of his soul,

But the stomach of the wicked shall be in want.

$tart the DVD $ession

(36 minutes)

Parallelisms and Personification

I. Parallelism

1. _____ poetry rhymes ideas rather than sounds most of the time. That's helpful — since we are reading it in English, we can "catch" a lot of the poetry despite the translation into English. Here are three types of parallelism or rhyming that occur in the Proverbs:

   A. **Synonymous parallelism** is perhaps the easiest to spot while reading.

2. This term applies to successive lines of text that state almost the _____ same thing. "The first line (or, stich) reinforc[es] the second and giving a distich (or, couplet)" (Unger 1951, p. 281).

   An example of this is found in Psalm 2:4:

   > He who sits in the heavens shall laugh; the Lord shall hold them in derision.

   B. The second type of parallelism, **synthetic parallelism**, is found when "the poet adds to the original concept" with ideas that 3. _____ on each other, adding additional color and meaning to the concept with each succeeding line.

   The first two verses of Psalm 1 are an example of this:

   > Blessed is the man
   >
   > Who walks not in the counsel of the ungodly,
   >
   > Nor stands in the path of sinners,
   >
   > Nor sits in the seat of the scornful;
   >
   > But his delight is in the law of the LORD,
   >
   > And in His law he meditates day and night.

4. Each successive line of this passage builds on the concept of what a man who is blessed will be like. Each of these phrases gives a little more _____ of what it means to be blessed.

C. Antithetic Parallelism

5. The third type of parallelism identified by Lowth is known as antithetic parallelism, which is nearly the opposite of _____ parallelism. This occurs when the second stich is directly contrasted to the first, and it is done to emphasize or confirm the thought of the first.

   Proverbs 15:2 provides a good example:

   > The tongue of the wise makes knowledge acceptable, but the mouth of fools spouts folly (NASB).

6. By _____ the folly from the mouth of fools with the tongue of the wise, it focuses attention on the rightness of the tongue of the wise.

Today's Proverb is Proverbs 13. It is one giant example of this third category, the antithetic parallelism, as it contrasts two concepts throughout: wisdom and foolishness — and it acts as a synthetic parallelism as it builds the concepts for each of them over and over.

II. Personification

7. The Proverbs often bring abstract concepts to life by giving them a _____.

   Wisdom and foolishness become "persons" through personification. The Bible introduces us to these characters of wisdom and foolishness as people so we can remember what to imitate and what to avoid.

So, let's do some personification that would apply to our culture. When you think of these two biblical characters, think of . . .

Andy Griffith was a strong Christian and was the voice of wisdom constantly in *The Andy Griffith Show*. Barney was silly, foolish, wise in his own eyes, and clueless. This is a good mental picture of what the writer of Proverbs 13 is describing.

Andy always had this common sense wisdom about life, conflict, difficulty, parenting, teaching hard work, money lessons with Opie, and you name it. Let's see how the whole passage (Proverbs 13:1–11) could be divided down the middle between our two characters.

	ANDY	BARNEY
1	A wise son heeds his father's instruction,	But a scoffer does not listen to rebuke.
2	A man shall eat well by the fruit of his mouth,	But the soul of the unfaithful feeds on violence.
3	He who guards his mouth preserves his life,	But he who opens wide his lips shall have destruction.
4	The soul of the diligent shall be made rich.	The soul of a lazy man desires, and has nothing;
5	A righteous man hates lying,	But a wicked man is loathsome and comes to shame.
6	Righteousness guards him whose way is blameless,	But wickedness overthrows the sinner.
7	And one who makes himself poor, yet has great riches.	There is one who makes himself rich, yet has nothing;
8	The ransom of a man's life is his riches,	But the poor does not hear rebuke.
9	The light of the righteous rejoices,	But the lamp of the wicked will be put out.
10	With the well-advised is wisdom.	By pride comes nothing but strife,
11	He who gathers by labor will increase.	Wealth gained by dishonesty will be diminished,

Notice how these categories are all divided between two characters: 8. _____and
9. _____.

See how foolishness leads to scoffing, wickedness, and poor use of your mouth and finances, while the voice of wisdom leads to life, light, good decisions, and truth talking.

Solomon has shown that these two characters approach everything differently, but there are three major categories in the passage that contrast Andy and Barney. Andy spends smarter because he practices three *contrasting skills* that Barney ignores:

1. Heeds versus feeds
2. Attention versus intention
3. Pretends to be poor versus pretends to be rich

I. Heeds Versus Feeds

1. A wise son *heeds* his father's instruction,　　But a scoffer does not listen to rebuke.

2. A man shall eat well by the fruit of his mouth,　　But the soul of the unfaithful feeds on violence.

3. He who guards his mouth preserves his life,　　But he who opens wide his lips shall have destruction.

10. The _____ man heeds, the scoffer feeds. The wise man heeds advice, and heeds the need for self-control for his lips, his temper, his spending, and his reaction.

11. The _____, Barney Fife, feeds himself excuses, rationalizations, victim talk, martyr talk, and he "feeds" on violence. And because of his foolishness, he lives and feeds off destruction.

12. Andy Griffith (wisdom) _____ instead of ignores. He doesn't mind "eating his words" since he had self-control in letting them out of his mouth. He can eat well. Andy knows that when you use self-control to guard your mouth, you save yourself a lot of pain.

13. Another word for foolish is to be _____.

II. Attention Versus Intention

14. Notice again the parallelism of Barney and Andy. Barney has a _____ soul who wants things, but has nothing because he doesn't implement his plans. While the soul (see the rhyming of ideas and words with the word "soul") of the diligent is made rich.

15. _____ has given attention to his actions, future, faith, and fortune. He gives attention to diligent spending guidelines and budgets. He diligently invests over time. He diligently puts into action the plans of his heart and mind.

16. The lazy man, Barney, "desires" or has _____ of dreaming, working, and motivating himself, but never really follows through with it.

17. God honors _____ investing over time

18. Barney, the wicked man, has intentions, without attention to the disciplines, diligence, and work needed to accomplish and work. He is loathesome and comes to _____.

19. Andy, the righteous man, hates _____. He moves forward diligently through honesty and integrity

TEST: Am I a Barney or an Andy?

Barneys say, "I have intentions of starting that."

Barneys say, "I haven't gotten to that yet."

Barneys say, "I have been too busy . . . and I don't have enough time."

Barneys say, "It would take too long or is outside my control."

Andys say, "I am putting my attention on making steps to move that way."

Andys say, "I am diligently giving attention to working one step at a time."

Andys say, "I am not a victim (being overthrown by my life), but I am giving attention to wisdom to be my fortress."

20. Barneys have a tendency to blame their _____, or think a goal is too far or too hard to pursue and become "overthrown in victimhood."

21. We give attention to our prayer life, our marriage, our time with kids, and our career —knowing _____ step at a time will get us there.

22. Isn't it amazing how both the fool and the _____ reside in us?

23. Giving _____ to God's word and statutes makes you more free and guarded by His wisdom.

Now we move into a section about money. Andy "pretends to be poor" while Barney "pretends to be rich."

III. Pretends to Be Poor Versus Pretends to Be Rich

There is one who makes himself rich, yet has nothing; And one who makes himself poor, yet has great riches (Proverbs 13:7).

24. At first glance you may not see what the writer is saying. The _____ "makes himself" (which means makes decisions) as if he is rich. He spends as if he is rich. He spends as if he doesn't have to budget or check his spending, as if he has all the money in the world. Yet he has nothing. He has debt. He has spent his savings. He has spent away money he could've given. He's spent on himself rather than on others. He has nothing.

25. Andy is one who "makes himself poor" by assuming that he has _____ than he really has. He spends less than he has so he can have savings and margin in life. Andy, by wisdom living, "pretends he is poor" so that he has riches through saving, giving, and investing in tomorrow.

The NLT says it this way:

Some who are poor pretend to be rich; others who are rich pretend to be poor.

A proverb later in chapter 21 reiterates the difference between pretending to be rich versus pretending to be poor:

There is desirable treasure, and oil in the dwelling of the wise, but a foolish man squanders it (Proverbs 21:20).

Pretending to be poor doesn't mean you can't get what you want. It means be 26. _____, thrifty, and 27. _____ in how you do it.

28. Thrift, generosity, resourcefulness, and creativity are unleashed within the confines of wisdom. Foolishness promises that you can _____ to afford things you can't, but you have nothing.

- No margin for emergencies
- No significant percentage for giving
- A whole bunch of debt to finance your "pretending to be rich"

29. _____ comes from ambition and 30. _____.

The ransom of a man's life is his riches, but the poor does not hear rebuke (Proverbs 13:8).

Here's where Solomon almost summarizes the main points between Barney and Andy: Foolishness and Wisdom.

Wisdom heeds God and doesn't need to pretend to be rich.

Foolishness feeds his self-indulgence and pretends to be rich but ends up in trouble.

The light of the righteous rejoices, But the lamp of the wicked will be put out.

By pride comes nothing but strife, But with the well-advised is wisdom.

Wealth gained by dishonesty will be diminished, But he who gathers by labor will increase (Proverbs 13:9–11).

$ettle the Discussion Questions

1. Who rules your heart? Andy or Barney? Wisdom or foolishness? Give examples.
2. Take the test "Am I a Barney or an Andy?" Make a list of your traits that resemble Barney and your traits that resemble Andy.

3. Pick one area to turn Barney into Andy:

Heeds versus feeds

Attention versus intention

Pretends to be poor versus pretends to be rich

Perhaps it's *heed versus feed*. How open are you to feedback? Do you seek out and listen when people give you feedback — constructive or otherwise? Do you heed their advice? This might be the one area you need to come against your inner Barney and become an Andy. And if you want this to be your own area — heed versus feed — you need God's grace.

Perhaps your one area to turn Barney into Andy is "attention versus intention." Maybe when you took that test, you thought, *I do procrastinate, make excuses, and put off what I know God has for me, my family, and my spiritual growth.* Commit today to moving from "intentions" (which are empty words) to "attention," by doing what God says, moving in His direction.

Perhaps your own area is "Pretend to be rich versus pretend to be poor." Perhaps you need to be wiser in your money by not buying, spending, or pursuing stuff that is beyond your reach. Some of us need a plan to undo the debt damage from all our pretending. Others of us need to start pretending to be "poorer" so we can be much, much more generous. We've "intended" to start giving a percentage of our income but we haven't given "attention to giving" an ever-increasing percentage of our income.

Start today. Start this week. Pick one area. Turn Barneys into Andys. Write out your plan.

$tudy the $ummary $tatement

Jesus is the ultimate source of wisdom, and He came to earth that through His wisdom He could confound the foolishness of the world. In fact, the Bible says God's foolishness is wiser than man's wisdom. And Jesus died for you and me, so we could be secure in our identity with Him.

When you are secure in your identity as a child of God, you are free from shame, guilt, and self-protection. Many of us don't really know this experientially. We can't "heed" constructive feedback because our souls still "feed" off idols for our security rather than feeding off His grace. When you feed off His grace, you can heed the voice of truth.

$tart the DVD $ession

(26 minutes)

$ee the Godly Perspective

Read the Book of Ruth.

$earch For Truth

Write a short essay on how Boaz demonstrates godly economics principles.

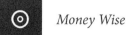
Create a Budget

Create a budget based around a take-home salary of $2,000 per month. Collect items for a budget portfolio: choose a job (self-employed or employed with a company), apartment to rent, public transport or making payments on a vehicle, utilities if not included in the rent, grocery lists and projected costs, insurance for glasses and dental if not part of work insurance, etc. Be sure to include incidental costs: clothing, shoes, pet care, insurance co-pays, entertainment like movies or DVD rentals or music subscriptions or purchases. Use newspaper and Internet ads (with permission) and visit stores to find real-world costs. Remember to pay your taxes! Write out your budget then have a parent review it for any items you may have missed.

Did you find it difficult to keep to your budget? What are some creative ways you can cut costs? What opportunities can you find that provide things you may want for free? Be creative and make a list of ways you have found to trim your budget but still enjoy the things you want.

Go a step further. What job did you choose? Does this job require an education or experience that you do not currently have? Write a life plan to achieve the goal of obtaining the job you chose.

Study the Stock Market

Choose ten stocks you feel would be a good investment and track their daily value over one month (by share price). You may use the NASE or NASDAQ values. Follow the news to see if trends related to new events or financial news releases from the company affect prices. Ask for permission to use the Internet. Create a chart to show the trends. What criteria did you use to select your stocks? If you had invested $1,000 in each stock, would you have made or lost money?

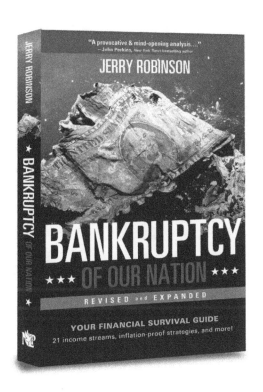

Economic Worksheets

for Use with

Bankruptcy of Our Nation

It has been said that
while history may never truly repeat,
it does at least rhyme.

Write a summary of the Introduction. Highlight the points important to the author, but also highlight the points that are of most interest to you.

1. America stands as the greatest _____ nation in world history.

2. Decades of financial excess, coupled with an _____ mentality, have left America financially bankrupt.

3. Over the last few decades, several economic trends have pointed toward an eventual day of _____ for the U.S. economy.

4. Our nation's _____, coupled with U.S. military adventurism since the Vietnam War era, has been largely financed by foreign creditors.

5. U.S. consumer _____ has reached all-time highs.

6. Since 1913, the Federal Reserve's excessive printing of the nation's currency has led to a 95 percent _____ in the dollar's value.

7. Since it was established as America's central bank in 1913, the Federal Reserve has operated without any meaningful congressional _____.

8. In _____, the United States led the entire global economy into a 100 percent paper money environment for the first time in world history.

9. The U.S. Constitution requires a declaration of war to be made by _____ prior to a military action.

10. No country can maintain its position in the global economy without developing a sustainable strategy for meeting its own _____ needs.

11. Write out the sequence of the world's great civilizations over about 200 years as described by Alexander Tyler:

12. Despite man's best efforts, _____ is still in control.

13. According to an orthodox view of the Christian faith, human suffering is rooted in man's rejection of the _____ rule of his Creator.

Write a summary of chapter 1. Highlight the points important to the author, but also highlight the points that are of most interest to you.

Short Aswers

What three factors has the author found that determine an individual's view of money?

1.

2.

3.

What four foundational questions need to be answered in order to understand the true impact of the global financial crisis, and how you can prepare yourself and even profit from it?

4.

5.

6.

7.

What are the three definitions of money?

8.

9.

10.

11. One of the first civilizations to develop a system of trade with a form of money was ancient

_____.

12. Give some examples of commodity money.

13. Describe the goldsmith banking system.

14. What is fractional-reserve banking?

15. What is fiat currency?

16. Describe how money is measured by U.S. economists under the four categories M0, M1, M2, and M3:

17. What exactly is it that gives the U.S. dollar its value?

18. How is paper money different from commodity money?

19. Today, all global currencies are issued by _____ and are controlled by an arrangement between governments and their central banks.

Write a Report

Write an essay on money. What is money? What gives money value? Compare and contrast the types of money used by countries around the world and how it is valued. Ask for permission before using the Internet for research.

Write a summary of chapter 2. Highlight the points important to the author, but also highlight the points that are of most interest to you.

Short Aswers

1. Why do fiat currency systems, like that of the U.S. dollar, demand an enormous amount of trust from the public in the monetary competency of their governments?

2. Is the U.S. dollar the first fiat (faith-based) currency in existence? And if it is not, what kind of historical track record do fiat currencies have? Are fiat currencies more likely to succeed or to fail?

3. Often, just prior to the demise of a fiat currency, the nation's economy appears to be experiencing widespread _____.

4. Despite his vast wealth, wisdom, and fame, the great king Solomon discovered that a life lived apart from the Creator was futile and that humanity's quest for meaning outside of God would always be _____.

5. While each historical case of fiat currency collapse is unique, it is all rooted in the same basic problem: human _____.

6. The more scarce the money supply, the _____ the price of the goods and services denominated in that currency.

7. The more abundant the money supply, the _____ the prices will be for the same goods and services.

8. What is hyperinflation?

9. What reasons are given for the fall of the Roman Empire?

10. What nation was the first to develop paper money?

11. Within _____ years of the introduction of paper money into the system, France and its citizens went from being impoverished to being fantastically wealthy (on paper), and then back into poverty again.

12. Who re-established a gold-backed monetary system in France to replace its failed paper money system, which led the country into an era of prosperity?

13. As was the case with most nations before them, Germany believed that it could overcome the rising prices by _____ even more money.

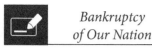
Short Aswers

14. How many examples of recent economic failure of the fiat system are listed by the author?

15. Pick your favorite warning issued regarding the fiat system and write it out:

16. _____ economy in the world uses a fiat currency!

17. Today's monetary systems are based and rooted in _____.

18. _____ has been defined as doing the same thing over and over again but expecting a different result.

19. Solutions are created only when enough people ask the question and demand an _____.

20. The larger the _____, the more severe the problems eventually become.

21. Over _____ verses of the Christian Bible contain a reference to money, wealth, and possessions.

22. Instead of denouncing fiat currencies, the Bible condemns what it calls "unjust _____ and balances."

23. Write out Proverbs 20:10.

24. A fiat currency system, in which the currency is backed by _____ and its value can be manipulated at will, is by definition an unjust weight.

25. Describe the differences between a 1923 one dollar bill (Silver Certificate) and a Modern U.S. dollar bill (Federal Reserve note).

26. George Washington and the Congress strongly detested paper currencies and therefore made special provisions within the act to ensure that anyone who attempted to debase the currency would be put to _____.

Write a summary of chapter 3. Highlight the points important to the author, but also highlight the points that are of most interest to you.

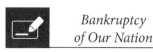

1. Explain the Bretton Woods system.

2. What three institutions were established in 1944 by the United Nations Monetary and Financial Conference?

   a.

   b.

   c.

3. What caused the economic devastation of Great Britain?

4. Why would Britain and all of these other nations be willing to allow the value of their currencies to be dependent upon the value of U.S. dollar?

5. List the four basic ways the U.S. government tries to solve its economic problems:

a.

b.

c.

d.

6. Printing money is the perfect solution for a country run by morally weak leaders who desperately want to avoid making any _____.

7. A monetary policy that relies upon the continued printing of money places the nation at great risk of huge _____.

8. Why is the U.S. dollar called a Federal Reserve note?

9. Who benefits from the continual global demand for dollars?

10. What president began a new federal government spending spree known as the Great Society program, a big government agenda that sought to provide new federal funding for public education, a so-called war on poverty, urban renewal, conservation, and crime prevention?

11. In addition to confronting a whole host of social issues, Johnson created what two new government-run systems?

12. While the United States was busy creating a large amount of handouts for its citizens, it was simultaneously waging an undeclared war in _____, at an estimated $5.1 billion per month.

13. How did the United States pay for its growing warfare and welfare state?

14. By 1971, as America's trade deficits increased and domestic spending soared, a growing number of nations who believed that the United States was abusing its leadership role within the global economy began publicly challenging the United States by demanding _____ in exchange for their dollar holdings.

15. Why didn't the United States prevent the breakdown of the Bretton Woods arrangement using the two available options suggested by the author?

16. In what year and under what president did the United States officially go under a fiat system?

17. What is a "floating" currency?

18. While this newfound monetary freedom would alleviate pressure on America's gold reserves, Washington was quick to recognize that this seismic shift in economic policy could eventually lead to a _____ global demand for the U.S. dollar.

Write a summary of chapter 4. Highlight the points important to the author, but also highlight the points that are of most interest to you.

1. What is a petrodollar?

2. The petrodollar system has motivated, and even guided, America's foreign policy in the _____ _____ for the last several decades.

3. Maintaining an _____ _____ _____ was vital if the United States were to continue expanding its welfare and warfare spending.

4. According to the agreement made with the Saudi royal family, the United States would offer military protection for Saudi Arabia's _____ fields.

5. What else did the United States also agree to provide the Saudis?

6. What two things did the Saudis agree to do for the United States?
   a.

   b.

7. By 1975, how many of the oil-producing nations of OPEC had agreed to price their oil in dollars and to hold their surplus oil proceeds in U.S. government debt securities in exchange for the generous offers by the United States?

8. What explains countries being eager to export affordable goods to the United States?

9. What three immediate benefits does the petrodollar system provide the United States?
   a.

   b.

   c.

10. What could cause hyperinflation in the United States? Why?

11. If the United States drastically reduces the supply of U.S. dollars to counter hyperinflation, what will happen to asset values?

12. The petrodollar system _____ demand for U.S. debt securities.

13. The petrodollar system also provides Washington with instant _____ for its debt securities, providing America with a double loan from virtually every global oil transaction.

14. Despite its obvious benefits, the petrodollar recycling process is both unusual and _____.

15. By distorting the real demand for government debt, it has "permitted" the U.S. government to maintain artificially low _____ rates.

Write a Report

Write a research report on how the petrodollar system has affected relations between the United States and Israel. What does the Bible say about how nations treat Israel? Ask for permission before using the Internet for research.

Write a summary of chapter 5. Highlight the points important to the author, but also highlight the points that are of most interest to you.

1. From the dawn of the petroleum age, developed nations have devised all sorts of creative geopolitical strategies to secure and maintain access to the world's _____ supplies.

2. In what year and under what U.S. president was the first official and formal commitment given to deploy U.S. troops to the Middle East for the explicit reason of protecting America's oil interests?

3. What was the stated mission of the Rapid Deployment Force (RDJTF)?

4. In what year and under what president did the Rapid Deployment Force morph into a separate force known as the United States Central Command (USCENTCOM), now responsible for the Middle East and Central Asian regions?

5. Why has the United States feverishly built hundreds of military bases (in over 130 countries) all over western Asia?

6. What are the four chief potential concerns for the petrodollar guardians, the United States?

    a.

    b.

    c.

    d.

7. Was there evidence linking Iraq to the 9/11 attacks to Iraq or its leader, Saddam Hussein, when Secretary of Defense Donald Rumsfield began ordering his staff to develop plans for a strike on Iraq?

8. Was the CIA able to find evidence linking Iraq to the terror attack of 9/11?

9. Government is not reason; it is not eloquent; it is _____. Like fire, it is a _____ servant and a fearful master. — President George Washington

10. According to both Clark and Engdahl, why did the United States appear so eager to launch an unprovoked war against Iraq? And why did the United States begin hatching these war plans many months prior to the events of September 11? After all, many other nations around the world have confirmed stockpiles of dangerous weapons. So why did the United States specifically target Iraq so soon after the Afghanistan invasion of 2001? Did the United States have some other motivation for seeking international support to invade Iraq? If so, what?

11. It should be noted that Iraq's proven oil supplies are considered to be among the _____ in the world.

12. Washington, of course, adamantly _____ any and all accusations that the Iraq war was motivated by anything other than disarming Iraq and liberating its beleagered people.

13. Based upon the quotes above, and upon the mountain of evidence that we have today, it is obvious that _____ had played some role in the U.S.-led Iraq invasion.

14. Name three nations that expressed opposition to the Iraqi invasion.

   a.

   b.

   c.

15. The opposing nations had existing oil contracts with Iraq that would be _____ in the event that the West gained control of Iraq.

16. Together with France and China, Russia stood to gain_____ in future oil contracts when, and if, sanctions were lifted against Iraq.

17. Within _____ of the invasion of Iraq, all Iraqi oil sales were switched from the euro — back to the U.S. dollar.

Write a summary of chapter 6. Highlight the points important to the author, but also highlight the points that are of most interest to you.

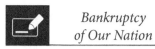
1. What did President Woodrow Wilson create on December 23, 1913?

2. The truth is that America's economic growth and prosperity has been made possible solely by
    _____.

3. Copy what John Adams had to say about coin, credit, and circulation:

4. While the British Crown could hardly impose strict religious adherence to their subjects across the Atlantic Ocean, they could exact _____ from the burgeoning American colonies.

5. On a diplomatic trip to England in 1763, Benjamin Franklin witnessed squalid living conditions in England. Franklin discovered that England was suffering from massive unemployment due to an exorbitantly high _____ burden upon its citizens.

6. What did Britain's Currency Act of 1764 attempt to do?

7. How long did it take America's streets to begin to resemble London's after the Currency Act was passed?

8. What act ultimately led to the Boston Tea Party?

9. Who was the first, and only, president to ever pay off the U.S. national debt?

10. What met Britain's attempts to confiscate its wealth through heavy taxes?

11. Who proposed a central bank in 1790?

12. Who was one of the opponents of the central banking system? Why did he oppose it? Write out his quote:

13. How do central banks manipulate the economies upon which they leech?

14. Why do many today believe that the fiat U.S. paper dollar is expressly forbidden by the U.S. Constitution?

15. Why do some people feel the Federal Reserve Bank is an unconstitutional institution?

16. Despite vehement opposition to the First Bank of the United States, President _____ _____ signed the First Bank of the United States into law on April 25, 1791, along with a 20-year charter, set to expire in 1811.

17. How much did the American government borrow from the First Bank during its first five years of operation? How much did prices rise during that time?

18. What right did Jefferson wish he could take from the federal government?

19. According to Gustavus Myers, who had a powerful influence in dictating American financial laws?

20. What bold threat did Rothschild make against the United States if the First Bank charter was not renewed?

21. Who funded the British in the War of 1812?

22. How did the war force the United States to charter the Second Bank of the United States?

23. Did President James Madison support the idea of private central banking?

24. What kind of cycles were brought on by the central bank?

25. What pitfall of the Second Bank did President Madison warn against? Write out his quote:

26. What five points did President Andrew Jackson give in opposition to the Second Bank of the United States?

    a.

    b.

    c.

    d.

    e.

27. Finish this quote by Andrew Jackson in response to Nicholas Biddle, president of the Second Bank: "That may be true, gentlemen, but that is your sin! Should I let you go on you will ruin fifty thousand families, and that would be my sin! You are a...."

28. When asked what his greatest accomplishment had been during his two terms as president, with what did Andrew Jackson reply and also order be engraved on his tombstone?

29. What was the period from 1837 to 1862 known as?

30. What was the deadliest war in American history?

31. Why did President Abraham Lincoln authorize the National Banking Act?

32. How did the National Banking Act differ from the First and Second Banks? Why are the differences important?

33. Copy the quote by John Sherman in his letter to New York bankers in regard to the 1863 National Banking Act:

34. Just before the passage of the National Banking Act, President Lincoln wrote a letter to William Elkin. Copy what Lincoln wrote:

35. What did Salmon P. Chase, the Secretary of the Treasury under Lincoln, express regarding his role in the passage of the National Banking Act?

36. What became the catalyst for the birth of the "Third" Bank of the United States?

37. The findings of the National Monetary Commission became the basis for what act?

38. From its inception, the Federal Reserve Bank was shrouded in _____.

39. Many Americans mistakenly believe that the Federal Reserve Bank is simply an agency of the federal government that is regulated at the federal level. However, this is not true. While it is true that the Federal Reserve was created by an act of Congress, the bank is not a _____entity.

40. The strict cloak of _____ under which the Federal Reserve was created should be _____ to all Americans.

41. What were the creators of the Federal Reserve hiding? Why did they feel such a strong need for secrecy? What was there to hide? (Copy Frank Vaderlip's quote.)

42. If monetary history has taught us anything it is that nations should cautiously guard who gains _____ over their money supply.

43. Copy what U.S. President James Garfield said a few weeks before his assassination in 1881:

44. Minnesota Congressman Charles A. Lindbergh said in 1913: "This [Federal Reserve Act] establishes the most gigantic trust on earth. When the President [Wilson] signs this bill, the invisible government of the monetary power will be legalized. . . . The worst legislative _____ of the ages is perpetrated by this banking and currency bill."

45. Why was the timing of the Senate vote on the proposed Federal Reserve Act quietly scheduled for the same week as Christmas break when many senators would have already gone home for the holiday?

46. What U.S. president signed the Federal Reserve Act into law?

47. The consolidation of the banking industry in 1921 allowed larger banks to purchase their former competitors for _____ on the dollar, giving more _____ to the nation's largest banks.

48. What was the "Roaring Twenties" marked by?

49. What month and year did the U.S. stock market drop precipitously, wiping out billions of dollars of American wealth in an instant and causing "bank runs," which led to the failure of over 10,000 banks?

50. What did the Federal Reserve do to prevent the crash and to stabilize the weakened economy?

51. What did the Executive Order 6102 issued by President Roosevelt authorize? What was the penalty for violating this order?

52. Who had seen the danger of the Great Depression coming and escaped the downturn?

53. Who would later openly express his concern that America was being controlled by a separate "invisible" government?

54. "We have restricted credit, we have restricted opportunity, we have controlled development, and we have come to be one of the worst _____, one of the most completely _____ and _____ governments in the civilized world…" -President Woodrow Wilson

55. How do international bankers make money according to Senator Barry Goldwater?

56. Copy the revealing comment made by Sir Josiah Stamp, the president of the Bank of England in the 1920s and the second richest man in Britain:

57. How did America lose the Revolutionary War?

58. Today, the U.S. government is heavily _____ to private banking interests — both domestic and foreign.

59. Who ultimately bears the responsibility for all of the debts incurred by our spendthrift government and their central banking schemes?

60. Instead of creating its own currency free of interest as it is instructed to do in Article I, Section VIII of the Constitution, it has chosen to _____ its own currency from the privately held Federal Reserve — at interest!

61. Our nation has become _____ to private banking interests and most do not even realize it.

Write a Report

Write a research report about Nelson Aldrich. Why is it significant that he was a friend of J.P. Morgan and father-in-law of John D. Rockefeller, Jr.? Who were these men and how have they affected the United States? Ask for permission before using the Internet for research.

Write a summary of chapter 7. Highlight the points important to the author, but also highlight the points that are of most interest to you.

1. Money is _____.

2. In what two ways does the U.S. government raise the money it needs to function?

    a.

    b.

3. When the government wants to borrow money, who does it turn to and how does that entity respond?

4. But what happens if the U.S. government wants to borrow more than the Treasury is able to sell in bonds?

5. Who controls the monetary policy of the U.S. federal government?

6. When the Fed purchases treasury bonds, where does it get the money?

7. U.S. currency is created out of government _____.

8. Who is the Fed owned by?

9. How does the Fed financially benefit from war?

10. What is the Fed's true incentive?

11. _____ perception is everything in modern politics and economics.

12. According to Article I, Section VIII of the U.S. Constitution, who is given sole power "to coin money, regulate the value thereof, and of foreign coin, and fix the Standard of Weights and Measures"?

13. In what year did a derelict U.S. Congress delegate their exclusive constitutional powers to coin and fix the standards of money to a private banking cartel?

14. The government's reckless borrowing from the Fed has subjected the American public to a new stealth tax called _____.

15. What issue imperils the entire American monetary system?

16. Why doesn't the government have the interest to pay back to the Fed?

17. The Federal Income Tax Code was passed in 1913 — the same year as the _____ _____.

18. A U.S. dollar bill says in big bold letters at the top and center: Federal Reserve _____.

19. A bank's primary purpose is to create money through _____.

20. The system of _____-_____ banking provides a far more powerful method from which banks can earn profits.

21. Fractional-reserve banking is a system that permits banks to keep only a "fraction" of customer deposits in reserve. Who determines what this "fractional" amount will be?

22. If the Fed is concerned that the economy is growing too quickly, it can _____ reserve requirement ratios, which will tighten the money supply as banks have less money to lend.

23. Why are the loans made by the bank considered assets and not liabilities? What key activity are banks allowed to do with their assets?

24. The bank has _____ percent, or less, of your deposited money at any one time.

25. Banks operate under the assumption that not every customer will need to _____ all of their money at the same time.

26. The _____ was designed to prevent future bank runs by guaranteeing the safety of most U.S. bank deposits, up to a total of $100,000.

27. A $100,000 deposit can be converted into _____ in new bank loans, created out of thin air.

28. In 2011, the FDIC announced that it was _____.

29. What happens when the debt owed on a bank loan is paid off?

30. "If there were no debts in the U.S. economy, there would be no _____."

31. Even if Americans agreed and voted to pay off the debt, it would be impossible. Why?

32. Sadly, the losers in our society face _____ and _____.

33. Copy the quote by Robert H. Hemphill, Credit Manager, Federal Reserve Bank, Atlanta, Georgia:

Write a summary of chapter 8. Highlight the points important to the author, but also highlight the points that are of most interest to you.

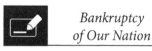
1. Copy Proverbs 22:7.

2. Who does the national debt belong to?

3. _____ _____ is an economic term for spending more than you earn.

4. What was Ronald Reagan's greatest disappointment of his presidency?

5. What absurd statement was made by President Bill Clinton on January 27, 1996?

6. How did the GOP rise to power in the 1990s?

7. The Republican-led "revolution" led to an _____ in government spending.

8. What happened to the national debt under George W. Bush?

9. What happened under former President Obama?

10. Americans have forgotten the most basic principles of liberty and have allowed our elected political leaders to ignore the proper role of government as set forth in our founding documents. America's founders envisioned an extremely _____ role for the federal government.

11. The primary reason for the astronomical increase in providing basic services to the U.S. population is due to a rise in government bureaucracies, which require a growing number of government _____.

12. One out of every _____ Americans is employed by the government sector, making it the largest employer of any industry in the national economy.

13. In 2010, the U.S. Senate conducted an investigation into government waste. In a rather embarrassing finding, they discovered that the federal government had been issuing payments to over 250,000 _____ Americans.

14. The leadership within both parties appears intent on continuing the _____ and _____ spending, despite the fact that doing so requires our country to borrow nearly $4 billion per day from total strangers.

15. How does the American public reward politicians who threaten to make draconian spending cuts?

16. The only true incentive that a modern U.S. politician has is getting _____.

17. It is difficult to lay all of the blame upon politicians when the actions of American _____ have helped reinforce their irresponsible behavior.

18. Instead of holding the political leaders accountable for doing nothing to solve our national crisis, the American public has sought to exploit politicians' perverse incentive structure for their own _____.

19. The American public has learned that they can vote themselves _____ through their local ballot box.

20. Name the top ten owners of our national debt:

21. For lovers of liberty and small government, it is a sad day as both Republicans and Democrats compete to _____ each other to appease our entitlement-crazed generation.

22. What did Albert Einstein reportedly call compound interest?

23. The White House anticipates that interest payments on the national debt will _____ over the next decade.

24. America's gargantuan debt is nothing less than a national _____ requiring immediate attention.

25. Mature adults learn to take _____ for their own actions.

Write a summary of chapter 9. Highlight the points important to the author, but also highlight the points that are of most interest to you.

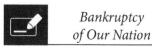

1. Who is Kathleen Casey-Kirschling?

2. Until recently, millions of baby boomers were the _____ payees into the Social Security and Medicare systems. That is, their payroll deductions were funding the benefit payments to current U.S. retirees.

3. From 2011 through 2030, 78 million baby boomers — or 10,000 people every single day — will retire and become financial and medical _____ of the current U.S. taxpayers.

4. America's unfunded liabilities on government entitlements alone are nearly _____ our entire national net worth!

5. What did the conservative think tank, the Heritage Foundation, call the looming entitlement crisis?

6. America's reckless overconsumption and addiction to credit represents a _____ issue.

7. Social Security is an _____ income transfer scheme where current benefit payouts are financed by the contributions made by current workers.

8. According to most projections, Social Security will remain solvent until around _____.

9. It is estimated that Medicare will become _____ sometime between 2016 and 2024.

10. U.S. policymakers have yet to create a _____ plan to prevent our entitlement crisis from wreaking havoc on the U.S. economy.

11. The Social Security Trust Fund is a double oxymoron: it is not "_____" and it should not be "_____."

12. If recent history is any indicator, it is highly probable that America's entitlement crisis will have to degenerate into total economic _____ before the politicians will even begin to discuss it seriously, let alone confront it.

13. In addition to facing an entitlement crisis, America has a _____ crisis to worry about.

14. How have many retirement-age Americans responded to all of this bad economic news?

Write a Report

Interview a family member or friend who will retire within the next five years. Find out what their financial plan is. Does it include Social Security? Do they plan to sell their home and buy a smaller one or rent? What are their plans for healthcare insurance? Do they believe Social Security and Medicare is solvent and will be there for the remainder of their life? What are their hopes and fears for their own future and for that of this nation? Write a report on your interview and how the views expressed are in agreement or disagreement of the projections stated in *Bankruptcy of Our Nation*.

Write a summary of chapter 10. Highlight the points important to the author, but also highlight the points that are of most interest to you.

1. The _____ power of the U.S. dollar has been declining, rather dramatically, for decades.

2. The problem with fiat currencies: the government can print them, as often as they like, with no _____.

3. The U.S. dollar is in a long-term downward _____ against other currencies.

4. The price of _____ is hitting an all-time high, as is the price of _____.

5. What three threads is the dollar's fate literally hanging by?

    a.

    b.

    c.

6. What are some of the nations who have been moving away from the dollar in their global oil transactions?

7. Name two of the primary beneficiaries of the new global search for higher rates of return:

    a.

    b.

8. Both Europe and China are aggressively seeking to create liquid government debt markets that will eventually _____ the United States in attracting global investment funds.

9. It is only a matter of time before another currency, considered to have more stability than the dollar, will be viewed as a viable _____ for the dollar in global trade.

10. In America today, we are living proof that having the world's most important _____ translates into a higher standard of living than most nations.

11. Today, America's largest _____ is the U.S. dollar.

12. What would happen if the artificial global dollar demand, made possible by the petrodollar system, were ever to crumble?

13. While it is likely no sane nation wants to _____ a dollar collapse, it is certain that no nation wants to be the last one holding the bag when it does collapse.

14. The life span of virtually every fiat currency has been around _____ years.

15. Every day _____ continues its out-of-control spending, it brings us one step closer to our nation's impending day of financial reckoning.

16. Without a strong dose of fiscal _____, coupled with political _____ and intestinal _____, the American social safety net that shields our nation's growing segments of the poor and the elderly will _____ before our eyes in the coming years.

17. What will cause America's financial demise?

18. The American people have been completely _____ by the corporate-controlled mainstream media.

19. Finding financial solutions that everyone can agree on is nearly impossible within a declining empire living in _____.

20. What have the most astute politicians rightly understood that the American public wants?

    a.

    b.

    c.

    d.

21. Raising taxes is the wrong solution because Washington does not have a revenue problem — it has a _____ problem.

22. Americans will continue to demand more benefits, not fewer, and any suggestions to cut spending for _____ will be met by a formidable boomer voting bloc.

23. The Federal Reserve has admitted that the entitlement crisis will be _____ through federal borrowing.

24. Our national obsession with avoiding any and all financial _____ will be our undoing.

25. Who is the largest single holder of our national debt?

26. Who is America's largest foreign creditor?

27. Foreign countries are no longer just questioning the wisdom of holding and hoarding U.S. debt instruments, but they are beginning to actively look for_____ .

Write a summary of chapter 11. Highlight the points important to the author, but also highlight the points that are of most interest to you.

1. Americans pride themselves on being a free people. But in reality, Americans are _____.

2. America's consumer debt levels have skyrocketed over the last several decades as corporations and the credit industry have worked hard to convince the entire collective culture that the "buy now, pay later" mentality will bring them _____.

3. Becoming "debt-free" in America is a complete _____.

4. Copy the quote on debt by President John Adams:

5. Some Americans become outraged when there is an inevitable increase in the cost of living without understanding that _____ will only continue to increase under our fiat monetary system.

6. Our nation's grand experiment with a debt-based monetary system is nearing its _____.

7. _____ has become a way of life for Americans as they have been programmed by the corporations, the credit industry, and the mass media to believe that happiness can only be found by having "more."

8. The concept of "more" has seeped into the halls of America's _____.

9. Unfortunately, for millions of Americans, excessive spending is a dangerous form of _____ designed to help them cope with the increasing amounts of stress caused by the American way of life.

10. Sadly, our nation has become so obsessed with consuming corporate goods and services that we have forgotten the practical wisdom and discipline of _____ even a small portion of our money.

11. _____ are the days of job stability and pension plans.

12. We are a nation dependent upon _____ and _____.

13. According to the current banking system of debt-based money, _____ are required.

14. Only those who can go out into the marketplace and find the _____ to pay back on their loans have a chance at coming out even.

15. There is never enough money in the system for everyone to pay back both principal and interest — because only the _____ exists.

16. What are the byproducts of our debt-based monetary system?

17. _____ is a stealth tax, and the fact that it is hidden makes it even more dangerous to your wealth potential.

18. What did the American economist Milton Friedman say about inflation?

19. Over the course of their working lifetimes, most American citizens will lose a large majority of their income to what three things?

   a.

   b.

   c.

20. Only through proper financial _____ can you even attempt to begin sheltering your wealth from all of the eroding factors on money.

Write a summary of chapter 12. Highlight the points important to the author, but also highlight the points that are of most interest to you.

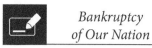
1. What three very powerful forces are currently working against your future wealth?

   a.

   b.

   c.

2. When consumption becomes _____, as it has in our modern era, the result can lead to financial devastation.

3. The Consumption Trap begins with _____.

4. Corporations seek marketing expertise for their products and services through _____ and _____ companies.

5. _____ institutions are in business to loan money to consumers for products and services that have been created by corporations and that are being promoted by the media.

6. Today, the Consumption Trap has convinced our society that _____ product and service that you use should be outsourced to corporations.

7. The "_____" are the ones in our society who are becoming wealthy in this entire process.

8. It is not going to get any _____ for those who want to rely upon corporations for every good and service that they consume.

9. Our modern producer-consumer system is _____ in human history.

10. Distinguish the difference between "_____" and "_____."

11. Drop the "_____ mentality" and adopt an "_____ mindset."

12. No one _____ you anything.

13. Begin _____ for yourself first, then for others.

14. Commit to developing _____ streams of income.

15. The Consumption Trap is real, but it does not have to _____ you and keep you from enjoying financial _____.

Quizzes and Tests Section

Money Wise Concepts & Comprehension	Quiz 1	Scope: Sessions 1–6	Total score: ____of 100	Name	

Questions (4 Points Each Question)

Three components of capitalism are:

1. _____

2. _____ (or liberty)

3. _____.

4. Capitalism does not eliminate _____, but it neutralizes it.

5. John Keynes ultimately moves you toward a _____ mindset.

6. *Godonomics* is based upon _____.

7. Keynesian economics is based upon _____.

8. Borrowing leads to _____.

9. A good man leaves an _____ to his children's children — Proverbs 15:22.

10. What caused the Great Depression? Deficit _____

11. What brought us out of the Great Depression? _____

12. Governments have no _____.

13. The value of money used to be tied to a _____. In America, the commodity was gold.

14. When President Woodrow Wilson wanted to print more money without getting more gold, he exchanged the commodity of gold for a _____ to make good economic decisions.

15. The Federal Reserve printed more money and therefore _____ the dollar.

16. The illusion of generosity means we measure or define generosity by our own _____ of what we are doing.

17. In America, liberty has led to _____, which has led to generosity.

18. Someone who works all day long but gets to take home none of his or her income is called a _____.

19. Government doesn't produce; it _____, enslaving us along the way.

20. All government purchases are _____ purchases.

21. The _____ became the motivating symbol to persuade Frenchmen to become a part of the new group and the new equality, because their rights did not come from God. Their rights came from the fraternity.

22. Coercive giving makes us more and more _____, rather than more and more cheerful.

23. _____ does not align with the Democrats nor the Republicans, but rather is a whole new way of thinking about money and economics.

24. President Franklin D. Roosevelt said that "the forgotten man" was the _____.

25. Amity Shlaes correctly demonstrates that the real forgotten man is the _____.

Questions (4 Points Each Question)

1. Capitalism is not just a good idea; it's _____ idea.

2. _____ celebrates work and profiting.

3. 2 Thessalonians: "If you do not work, you don't _____."

4. Money is not unproductive or wrong. The Greek idea of _____ taught that the world was inherently bad, that matter was bad.

5. Profiting honors God and inspires others. Doing your work with _____, whatever it is, honors God.

When Christians realize that profits are good, but not enough, they begin to 6. _____ differently and 7. _____ differently.

8. Enjoy profits without being _____to them.

9. The _____ is key in moving people, especially children, but also employees because you want to mark the values into their heart in such a way they will "own the values" and "defend the values."

10. Employees who work for a _____ agree when the boss is in the room.

Jesus engaged the hearts of His 11. _____, the ones killing Him, by saying, "Father, 12. _____ them, for they know not what they do."

13. Generosity increases _____.

14. Generosity decreases _____.

15. In the Garden, we are introduced to a God who _____.

There are two temptations that weaken work: The tendencies to 16._____ and

17. _____.

The role of government, or the king, according to the Bible, is to enforce the 18. _____ of 19. _____.

Prime time is about injecting 20. _____ into your 21. _____. Time is limited, but not as limited as your energy.

22. Our _____ time is that time in our day that is NOT our ideal creative, productive, best time, but the "get through the details" time that we all need to do weekly.

23. You never, ever get more time, so instead we convert *chronos* into *kairos* by turning minutes into _____.

24. God's _____ is a rhythm of rest, productivity, creativity, and relationship.

25. God honors _____ investing over time.

Questions (3 Points Each Question)

1. America stands as the greatest _____ nation in world history.

2. Since 1913, the Federal Reserve's excessive printing of the nation's currency has led to a 95 percent _____ in the dollar's value.

3. What are the three definitions of money?

   a.

   b.

   c.

4. What is fractional-reserve banking?

5. What is hyperinflation?

6. A fiat currency system, in which the currency is backed by _____ and its value can be manipulated at will, is by definition an unjust weight.

7. What three institutions were established in 1944 by the United Nations Monetary and Financial Conference?

   a.

   b.

   c.

8. Why is the U.S. dollar called a Federal Reserve note?

9. In what year and under what president did the United States officially go under a fiat system?

10. What is a petrodollar?

11. What three immediate benefits does the petrodollar system provide the United States?

    a.

    b.

    c.

12. If the United States drastically reduces the supply of U.S. dollars to counter hyperinflation, what will happen to asset values?

13. According to both Clark and Engdahl, why did the United States appear so eager to launch an unprovoked war against Iraq?

14. What did President Woodrow Wilson create on December 23, 1913?

15. What did John Adams have to say about coin, credit, and circulation?

16. Who was the first, and only, president to ever pay off the U.S. national debt?

17. Why do many today believe that the fiat U.S. paper dollar is expressly forbidden by the U.S. Constitution?

18. What bold threat did Rothschild make against the United States if the First Bank charter was not renewed?

19. When asked what his greatest accomplishment had been during his two terms as president, with what did Andrew Jackson reply and also order to be engraved on his tombstone?

20. From its inception, the Federal Reserve Bank was shrouded in _____.

21. Why was the timing of the Senate vote on the proposed Federal Reserve Act quietly scheduled for the same week as Christmas break when many senators would have already gone home for the holiday?

22. What U.S. president signed the Federal Reserve Act into law?

23. The consolidation of the banking industry in 1921 allowed larger banks to purchase their former competitors for _____ on the dollar, giving more _____ to the nation's largest banks.

24. Who had seen the danger of the Great Depression coming and had escaped the downturn?

25. How did America lose the Revolutionary War?

26. Our nation has become _____ to private banking interests, and most do not even realize it.

Each Question Worth 5 Points

27. Explain the Bretton Woods system.

28. How do central banks manipulate the economies upon which they leech?

Each Question Worth 6 Points

29. Describe the goldsmith banking system.

30. What is fiat currency?

Questions (4 Points Each Question)

1. Money is _____.

2. When the government wants to borrow money, who does it turn to, and how does that entity respond?

3. What issue imperils the entire American monetary system?

4. Even if Americans agreed and voted to pay off the debt, it would be impossible. Why?

5. Who does the national debt belong to?

6. Americans have forgotten the most basic principles of liberty and have allowed our elected political leaders to ignore the proper role of government as set forth in our founding documents. America's founders envisioned an extremely _____ role for the federal government.

7. The leadership within both parties appears intent on continuing the _____ and _____ spending, despite the fact that doing so requires our country to borrow nearly $4 billion per day from total strangers.

8. What did Albert Einstein reportedly call compound interest?

9. What did the conservative think tank, the Heritage Foundation, call the looming entitlement crisis?

10. According to most projections, Social Security will remain solvent until around _____.

11. The Social Security Trust Fund is a double oxymoron: it is not "_____" and it should not be "_____."

12. How have many retirement-age Americans responded to all of this bad economic news?

13. The _____ power of the U.S. dollar has been declining, rather dramatically, for decades.

14. Name two of the primary beneficiaries of the new global search for higher rates of return:

15. What will cause America's financial demise?

16. What have the most astute politicians rightly understood that the American public wants?
    a.

    b.

    c.

    d.

17. _____ has become a way of life for Americans as they have been programmed by the corporations, the credit industry, and the mass media to believe that happiness can only be found by having "more."

18. Unfortunately, for millions of Americans, excessive spending is a dangerous form of _____ designed to help them cope with the increasing amounts of stress caused by the American way of life.

19. Sadly, our nation has become so obsessed with consuming corporate goods and services that we have forgotten the practical wisdom and discipline of _____ even a small portion of our money.

20. _____ is a stealth tax, and the fact that it is hidden makes it even more dangerous to your wealth potential.

21. Name two of the three very powerful forces that are currently working against your future wealth.

22. The "_____" are the ones in our society who are becoming wealthy in this entire process.

23. Our modern producer-consumer system is _____ in human history.

24. Distinguish the difference between "_____" and "_____."

25. Drop the "_____ mentality" and adopt an "_____ mindset."

_____

	Money Wise	Test 1	Scope:	Total score:	Name
	Concepts & Comprehension		Sessions 1–14	____of 100	

Questions (5 Points Each Question)

Three components of capitalism are:

1. _____

2. _____ (or liberty)

3. _____.

4. John Keynes ultimately moves you toward a _____ mindset.

5. *Godonomics* is based upon _____.

6. Keynesian economics is based upon _____.

7. Borrowing leads to _____.

8. What caused the Great Depression? Deficit _____

9. What brought us out of the Great Depression? _____

10. The illusion of generosity means we measure or define generosity by our own _____ of what we are doing.

11. Capitalism is not just a good idea; it's _____ idea.

12. Money is not unproductive or wrong. The Greek idea of _____ taught that the world was inherently bad, that matter was bad.

13. Profiting honors God and inspires others. Doing your work with _____, whatever it is, honors God.

14. Enjoy profits without being _____to them.

Jesus engages the hearts of His 15. _____, the ones killing Him, by saying, "Father,
16. _____ them for they know not what they do."

17. Generosity increases _____.

18. Generosity decreases _____.

There are two temptations that weaken work: The tendencies to

19. _____ and

20. _____.

| *Bankruptcy of Our Nation* | Test 1 | Scope: | Total score: | Name |
| Concepts & Comprehension | | Chapters 1–12 | ____of 100 | |

Questions (5 Points Each Question)

1. What are the three definitions of money?

2. What is fractional-reserve banking?

3. What is hyperinflation?

4. What three institutions were established in 1944 by the United Nations Monetary and Financial Conference?

5. What is a petrodollar?

6. How did America lose the Revolutionary War?

7. Explain the Bretton Woods system.

8. How do central banks manipulate the economies upon which they leech?

9. Describe the goldsmith banking system.

10. What is fiat currency?

11. Money is _____.

12. Even if Americans agreed and voted to pay off the debt, it would be impossible. Why?

13. Who does the national debt belong to?

14. The leadership within both parties appears intent on continuing the _____ and _____ spending, despite the fact that doing so requires our country to borrow nearly $4 billion per day from total strangers.

15. What did the conservative think tank, the Heritage Foundation, call the looming entitlement crisis?

16. The Social Security Trust Fund is a double oxymoron: it is not "_____" and it should not be "_____."

17. What will cause America's financial demise?

18. Sadly, our nation has become so obsessed with consuming corporate goods and services that we have forgotten the practical wisdom and discipline of _____ even a small portion of our money.

19. Name two of the three very powerful forces that are currently working against your future wealth.

20. Distinguish the difference between "wants" and "_____."

| Economics | Final | Scope: | Total score: | Name |
| Concepts & Comprehension | Test | Final | ____of 100 | |

Questions (5 Points Each Question)

Three components of capitalism are:

1. _____

2. _____ (or liberty)

3. _____.

4. John Keynes ultimately moves you toward a _____ mindset.

5. Borrowing leads to _____.

6. What caused the Great Depression? Deficit _____

7. What brought us out of the Great Depression? _____

8. Profiting honors God and inspires others. Doing your work with _____, whatever it is, honors God.

9. Enjoy profits without being _____to them.

10. Generosity increases _____.

11. What is fractional-reserve banking?

12. What is a petrodollar?

13. How did America lose the Revolutionary War?

14. How do central banks manipulate the economies upon which they leech?

15. Describe the goldsmith banking system.

16. What is fiat currency?

17. Money is _____.

18. What will cause America's financial demise?

19. Sadly, our nation has become so obsessed with consuming corporate goods and services that we have forgotten the practical wisdom and discipline of _____ even a small portion of our money.

20. Distinguish the difference between "_____" and "needs."

21) liberty

22) security

23) money

24) security

25) liberty

26) refused to obey

27) taxed

28) limited

29) government

30) Jesus

Discussion Questions: Answers will vary but should be thoughtful and show an understanding of the material.

Session Four, Worksheet 2

1) Value

2) dishonest

3) commodity

4) promise

5) Federal

6) Reserve

7) money

8) inflation

9) results

10) devalued

11) Abundance

12) hoarding

13) overspending

14) entitlement

15) coveting

16) discontent

17) greed

18) yourself

19) God

20) generosity

21) standard

22) 2

23) organizing

24) lavishly

25) generous

26) sacrifice

Discussion Questions: Answers will vary but should be thoughtful and show an understanding of the material.

Show Support Question: Answers will vary.

Session Five, Worksheet 2

1) freedom

2) more

3) control

4) America

5) two

6) liberty

7) sixth

8) fourth

9) New Jersey

10) prosperity

11) freedom

Session Five, Worksheet 3

13) The Scale

14) choices

15) standard of living

16) slave

17) freedom

18) wealth

19) poverty

20) socialism

21) richest

22) 10th

23) consumes

24) The Purchase

25) price

26) quality

27) First-party

28) unfair

29) price

30) Second-party

31) Third-party
32) third-party
33) enjoy the benefits
34) Tear
35) down
36) bless

Session Five, Worksheet 4

37) The Worldview
38) individually
39) life
40) liberty
41) happiness
42) property
43) guillotine
44) fasting
45) prayer
46) worship
47) teach
48) nation

Discussion Questions: Answers will vary but should be thoughtful and show an understanding of the material.

Show Support Question: Answers will vary.

Session Six, Worksheet 2

1) political
2) religious
3) bitter
4) *Godonomics*
5) Lower
6) stimulate
7) increased
8) higher
9) taxes
10) less
11) taxes
12) poor/needy
13) producer
14) give
15) coerce

16) force
17) Coercion
18) Cheerfully
19) grace
20) motivator
21) produce
22) leverage
23) doesn't
24) work
25) greed
26) free
27) prosperous
28) generous

Discussion Questions: Answers will vary but should be thoughtful and show an understanding of the material.

Session Seven, Worksheet 2

1) God's
2) set
3) portrait
4) purpose
5) self
6) customer
7) society
8) Creator
9) God
10) God
11) yourself
12) incentive
13) freedom
14) uniquely
15) eat
16) rewarding
17) others
18) paycheck
19) career
20) bless
21) society
22) impact/change

23) dualism

24) calling

25) spiritual

26) worship

27) Creator

28) reason

29) purpose

30) mask

Discussion Question: Answers will vary but should be thoughtful and show an understanding of the material.

Session Eight, Worksheet 2

1) Enough

2) competence

3) competence

4) excellence

5) competence

6) Bible

7) excellence

8) competence

9) accuracy

10) celebrate

11) pay

12) profit

13) fair

14) market

15) Golden

16) Rule

17) profits

18) everything

19) values

20) enslaved

Discussion Questions: Answers will vary but should be thoughtful and show an understanding of the material.

Show Support Question: Answers will vary.

Session Nine, Worksheet 2

1) Leaders

2) three

3) engage

4) mind

5) cupbearer

6) middle

7) how

8) Nehemiah

9) community

10) cause

11) corporation

12) heart

13) ownership

14) hearts

15) embed

16) cast

17) vision

18) paycheck

19) Millenials/Gen Xers

20) Nehemish

21) simple

22) sticky

23) exactly

24) enemies

25) forgive

Discussion Questions: Answers will vary but should be thoughtful and show an understanding of the material.

Session Ten, Worksheet 2

1) examine

2) rhythm

3) unique

4) redeem

5) energy

6) time

7) 30

8) best

9) protect

10) crank

11) through

12) grime
13) *chronos*
14) *kairos*
15) minutes
16) opportunities
17) moments
18) buy
19) back
20) high
21) priority
22) medium
23) low
24) prioritizing
25) wise
26) will
27) dynamics
28) in it
29) on it
30) declutter

Session Ten, Worksheet 3

Discussion Question: Answers will vary but should be thoughtful and show an understanding of the material.

Session Ten, Worksheet 4

Answers will vary.

Session Eleven, Worksheet 2

1) curiosity
2) animosity
3) followers
4) gives
5) community
6) creativity
7) generosity
8) works
9) human
10) work
11) evil
12) forgiven

13) private
14) property
15) socialism
16) Scripture
17) Ten
18) Commandments
19) incentive
20) steward
21) generosity
22) parties
23) pillar
24) smoke
25) curiosity
26) context
27) Church
28) others
29) longsuffering
30) patience

Discussion Questions: Answers will vary but should be thoughtful and show an understanding of the material.

Session Twelve, Worksheet 2

1) isolate
2) insulate
3) law
4) Lemuel
5) justice
6) poor
7) rule
8) law
9) fair
10) trials
11) property
12) rights
13) weaken
14) virtuous
15) supportive
16) lacking

17) investor

18) merchant

19) ship

20) God's

21) provide

22) work

23) loving

24) profiting

25) commerce

26) poor/needy

27) Bible

28) God

29) Lord

Discussion Questions: Answers will vary but should be thoughtful and show an understanding of the material.

Session Thirteen, Worksheet 2

1) Hebrew

2) exact

3) build

4) details

5) synonymous

6) contrasting

7) personality

8) wisdom

9) foolishness

10) wise

11) scoffer

12) heeds

13) unfaithful

14) lazy

15) Andy

16) intentions

17) diligently

18) shame

19) lying

20) circumstances

21) one

22) wise

23) attention

24) fool

25) less

26) creative

27) resourceful

28) pretend

29) Contentment

30) thriftiness

Discussion Questions: Answers will vary but should be thoughtful and show an understanding of the material.

Session Fourteen, Worksheet 1

Answers will vary.

Introduction, Worksheet 1

Summary—The student's summary will vary but
    should show the chapter has been read and the
    student understands the material.

Introduction, Worksheet 2

1) debtor

2) entitlement

3) reckoning

4) overconsumption

5) debt

6) decrease

7) oversight

8) 1971

9) Congress

10) energy

11) These nations have progressed through the
    following sequence:

    from bondage to spiritual faith,

    from spiritual faith to great courage,

    from courage to liberty,

    from liberty to abundance,

    from abundance to selfishness,

    from selfishness to complacency,

    from complacency to apathy,

    from apathy to dependency,

    from dependency back to bondage.

12) God

13) omnipotent

Chapter One, Worksheet 1

Summary—The student's summary will vary but
    should show the chapter has been read and the
    student understands the material. Some of the
    following points should be included:

- Our own personal view of money is shaped and
  influenced by three factors: 1) the economic
  system we are born into, 2) our family's
  financial philosophy, and 3) our instilled
  spiritual and moral values.

- Money is morally neutral. It can be used for

positive or negative reasons. Financial morality
is found in the intentions of the user, not in the
money itself.

- Three forms of money have been used
  throughout history: 1) commodity money,
  2) receipt money, 3) fiat money

- Commodity money took the form of
  exchangeable commodities, often with intrinsic
  value such as salt, livestock, and crops.

- Along with the advance of civilizations
  came the need for a form of money that was
  relatively scarce, portable, easily divisible, and
  durable.

- Precious metals, such as gold and silver, fit all of
  these requirements, making them the obvious
  choice.

- Over time, goldsmith banking allowed
  individuals a safe place to store their gold
  in exchange for a paper receipt that was
  considered as "good as gold."

- These paper receipts, or receipt money, were
  extremely popular due to their ease of use.

- The governing authorities eventually saw a
  need to monopolize the money-creation process
  in order to ensure economic stability.

- This government intervention led to the rise of
  central banks and fiat monetary systems that
  have ultimately proven to be disastrous.

- Fiat money has no intrinsic value. Instead, its
  value is derived from legal tender laws and a
  public perception that the monetary authorities
  will keep it in a limited supply.

- Today, every currency on the planet is
  considered to be fiat.

Chapter One, Worksheet 2

1) the economic system into which the person is
   born

2) the financial philosophy espoused by his family

3) their religious and moral understanding of life
   itself

4) What is money?

5) How is money measured?

6) What gives money its value?

7) If money can be printed to prevent a financial crisis, why not just print more?

8) Money is . . . a medium of exchange

9) Money is . . . a store of value

10) Money is . . . a unit of account

11) Sumer

12) spearheads, shells, feathers, and salt

13) Under the goldsmith banking system, which became popular in 17th-century England, a person would simply deposit his gold with his local goldsmith. Much like modern banking, the goldsmith would provide the depositor with a paper receipt stating the amount of gold on deposit. If the person wanted to redeem his gold, he simply returned his paper receipt to the goldsmith. (In exchange for this convenience of keeping the gold in a safe place, the town's goldsmith would charge a small monthly maintenance fee.)

14) Lending money not currently on deposit.

15) When a nation detaches its paper currency system from any and all commodity backing, its currency is then considered by economists to be a fiat currency. When a currency is issued by fiat, it is backed only by government guarantees, not a commodity. Fiat money has no intrinsic value. Its value is derived strictly by government law, and unlike the first two types of money (commodity and receipt) there is no natural limit to the quantity of fiat money that can be produced.

16) M0 Money Supply: This measurement includes all coin and paper currency in circulation, as well as accounts at the central bank that can be exchanged for physical currency. This is the narrowest measure of the U.S. money supply and only measures the amount of liquid money in the hands of the public and certain deposits with the Federal Reserve.

M1 Money Supply: This measurement includes everything in M0 as well as currency held in demand deposits (such as checking accounts and NOW accounts) and traveler's checks (which can be liquidated into physical currency).

M2 Money Supply: This category includes everything in M1, plus all of the currency held in saving accounts, money market accounts, and certificates of deposit with balances of $100,000 or less.

M3 Money Supply: As the broadest measure of the U.S. money supply, this category combines all of M2 (which includes M1) plus all currency held in certificates of deposit with balances over $100,000, institutional money market funds, short-term repurchase agreements, and eurodollars (U.S. dollars held in foreign bank accounts).

17) Faith in the scarcity of the dollar.

18) It has no intrinsic value.

19) fiat

Chapter Two, Worksheet 1

Summary—The student's summary will vary but should show the chapter has been read and the student understands the material. Some of the following points should be included:

- Fiat currencies require an enormous amount of faith and trust in the monetary authorities by the public.

- Inflation is defined as an increase in a nation's money supply.

- Hyperinflation occurs when a nation's money supply becomes out of control.

- Every fiat currency devised throughout history has faced the same embarrassing and miserable death: utter collapse by overproduction.

- While the landscape of world history is littered with failed fiat currencies, history is also replete with warnings from our ancestors regarding the inherent dangers of fiat currencies.

- Biblically speaking, fiat currencies are modern versions of "unjust weights" and "false balances."

Chapter Two, Worksheet 2

1) Because the future value of a fiat currency is entirely dependent upon the financial wisdom and vigilant oversight of the nation's monetary authorities in keeping the currency in a limited and strictly measured supply.

2) The U.S. dollar is not the first fiat currency in history. Every fiat currency devised throughout history has faced the same embarrassing and

miserable death: utter collapse by overproduction. The fact that so many currency collapses throughout history were initiated under the auspices of "good intentions" should be a cause for concern to all who distrust the true motives of the monetary authorities in our modern era.

3) prosperity

4) fruitless

5) greed

6) lower

7) higher

8) When an increase in a nation's money supply, or inflation, becomes uncontrollable, it is called hyperinflation. Hyperinflation is one of the most dangerous economic problems that can confront a nation as it causes dramatic price increases which eventually cripple the underlying economy.

9) significant government overspending, financial greed, an entitlement mentality, and military overextension.

10) China

11) four

12) Napoleon Bonaparte

13) printing

Chapter Two, Worksheet 3

14) fourteen

15) Answers will vary.

16) Every

17) debt

18) Insanity

19) answer

20) government

21) 2,350

22) weights

23) "Diverse weights and diverse measures, they are both alike, an abomination to the Lord."

24) nothing

25) The 1923 U.S. dollar says at the top of the bill: Silver Certificate: This certifies that there has been deposited in the treasury of the United States of America. Toward the bottom of the bill it states: One silver dollar payable to the bearer on demand. (The owner of this dollar bill could trade it in at any time for one dollar's worth of silver. In 1923, the dollar was a form of receipt money which could be redeemed in a fixed rate for gold or silver.)

On the modern U.S. dollar the language on the front of this U.S. dollar bill has changed. At the top, it simply states: Federal Reserve Note. At the bottom, the language has changed from One Silver Dollar payable to the bearer on demand to simply One Dollar.

26) death

Chapter Three, Worksheet 1

Summary—The student's summary will vary but should show the chapter has been read and the student understands the material. Some of the following points should be included:

- The devastation of the global economic order in the wake of World War II led world leaders to form a conference to create solutions. This conference, known as Bretton Woods, led to the creation of a new global fixed exchange rate regime with the U.S. dollar playing a central role.

- Under the Bretton Woods system, an ounce of gold could be purchased at a fixed international rate of $35 per ounce. Because this fixed rate was regulated, the U.S. dollar was considered "as good as gold."

- This new international "dollars for gold" system created under Bretton Woods restored global economic stability to war-weary economies. As a result, foreign nations pegged their currencies to the dollar with the ability to convert their dollar holdings to gold at any time.

- In the late 1960s, the Bretton Woods system broke down as foreign nations cashed in their dollars for gold. This was largely due to global concern over Washington's reliance upon deficit spending to fund its warfare and welfare policies.

- On August 15, 1971, President Richard Nixon closed the international gold window, which ended the Bretton Woods system and the dollar's convertibility to gold. It was on this day that virtually every global currency became fiat, with no commodity backing.

Chapter Three, Worksheet 2

1) The U.S. dollar would be linked to gold at a pre-determined fixed rate of $35 per ounce. In turn, all other currencies were then pegged to the dollar, as it was viewed as being as "good as gold." This immediate convertibility from U.S. dollars into a fixed amount of gold brought much-needed economic relief and helped to restore confidence in the global financial markets.

2) a. The World Bank

b. The International Monetary Fund (IMF)

c. The World Trade Organization (originally called the General Agreement on Trades and Tariffs, or GATT)

3) military overextension and economic arrogance

4) They didn't really have a choice. These war-weary nations were broke. And there was literally no other currency, outside of the dollar, that was able to fill the growing demands of the global economic system.

5) a. Increase income by raising taxes on the citizens

b. Cut government spending by reducing public benefits

c. Borrow money through the issuance of government bonds

d. Print money

6) sacrifices

7) inflation

8) The U.S. Dollar is issued and loaned to the United States government by the Federal Reserve Bank.

9) The U.S. government benefits from the ability to create money out of thin air. Politicians benefit as global dollar demand gives them a convenient way to finance their excessive spending. U.S. citizens benefit from rising asset prices, although these are tempered by the creeping amounts of inflation created through such money printing. However, by far the largest beneficiary of global dollar demand is

America's central bank, the Federal Reserve. If this does not make immediate sense, then pull out a dollar bill from your wallet or purse and notice whose name is plastered right on the top of it.

10) Lyndon B. Johnson

11) Medicare and Medicaid

12) Vietnam

13) It simply borrowed the money, also known as deficit spending.

14) gold

15) They both required fiscal restraint and economic responsibility. Then, as now, there was very little appetite for reducing consumption in the name of "sacrifice" or "responsibility."

16) 1971, Richard Nixon

17) It is a currency that is not fixed in value.

18) declining

Chapter Four, Worksheet 1

Summary—The student's summary will vary but should show the chapter has been read and the student understands the material. Some of the following points should be included:

- A petrodollar is a U.S. dollar that is received by an oil producer in exchange for selling oil and that is then deposited into Western banks.

- The artificial demand that had been created, and then lost, under the Bretton Woods system was restored to even higher levels under the petrodollar system.

- The petrodollar system was one of the most clever political strategies of the 20th century.

- Four primary benefits to America from the petrodollar system include: 1) an artificial demand for dollars, 2) an artificial demand for U.S. government debt, 3) the ability to print the currency in which oil must be purchased, and 4) an influx of cheap imported goods from foreign nations who need our dollars to purchase oil.

- When a country does not have a surplus of U.S. dollars, it must create a strategy to obtain them in order to buy oil. This helps to explain the adoption of export-led strategies by several resource-poor nations, particularly in the Far East.

Chapter Four, Worksheet 2

1) A petrodollar is a U.S. dollar that is received by an oil producer in exchange for selling oil and that is then deposited into Western banks.

2) Middle East

3) artificial dollar demand

4) oil

5) military assistance, weapons, and perhaps most importantly, protection from Israel's growing military arsenal.

6) a. The Saudis must agree to price all of their oil sales in U.S. dollars only.

   b. The Saudis would be open to investing their surplus oil proceeds in U.S. debt securities.

7) all of them

8) They need U.S. dollars to buy oil.

9) a. It increases global demand for U.S. dollars

   b. It increases global demand for U.S. debt securities

   c. It gives the United States the ability to buy oil with a currency it can print at will

10) If the petrodollar system collapses it will decrease demand for the dollar. When this occurs, the amount of dollars in existence will far exceed the actual demand, causing hyperinflation.

11) There will be a massive reduction in asset value.

12) increases

13) buyers

14) unsustainable

15) interest

Chapter Five, Worksheet 1

Summary—The student's summary will vary but should show the chapter has been read and the student understands the material. Some of the following points should be included:

- A proper understanding of the petrodollar system helps explain why there are hundreds of U.S. military bases stationed in over 130 countries.

- In order to protect the petrodollar system, the United States must be vigilant to deal with 1) threats to restrictions on oil supplies, 2) new oil discoveries in potentially "anti-Western" oil fields, 3) the nationalizing of a country's oil supplies, and 4) devising "permanent solutions" to the problems presented by nations who dare challenge the current "dollars for oil" system.

- On September 24, 2000, Iraqi President Saddam Hussein boldly determined to remove all of his oil sales away from the U.S. dollar and began accepting euros for his country's oil supplies in 2002.

- On March 19, 2003, the U.S. military invaded Iraq under false pretext. The American media provided a scarce amount of critical reporting.

- On June 5, 2003, Iraq's oil sales were returned to the petrodollar system.

- When pressed, U.S. politicians admit that our wars are often motivated by natural resources.

Chapter Five, Worksheet 2

1) oil

2) 1973, President Richard Nixon

3) a deterrent (primarily against the Soviets) and to "help maintain regional stability and the Gulf oil-flow westward."

4) 1983, President Jimmy Carter

5) to maintain an empire dependent upon a "dollars for oil" system, which is no cheap task, and requires careful monitoring and oversight of the world's oil supplies.

6) a. threats of restrictions on oil supplies,

   b. new oil discoveries in potentially "anti-Western" oil fields,

   c. the nationalizing of a country's oil supplies, and perhaps most importantly,

   d. devising "permanent solutions" to the problems presented by nations who dare challenge the current "dollars for oil" system.

7) no

8) no

9) force, dangerous

10) The U.S.-led invasion was inspired predominantly by Iraq's public defiance of the

petrodollar system. According to page 28 of Clark's book: On September 24, 2000, Saddam Hussein allegedly "emerged from a meeting of his government and proclaimed that Iraq would soon transition its oil export transactions to the euro currency." By 2002, Saddam had fully converted to a petroeuro — in essence, dumping the dollar.

11) largest

12) denied

13) oil

14) China, Russia, and France

15) endangered

16) billions

17) weeks

Chapter Six, Worksheet 1

Summary—The student's summary will vary but should show the chapter has been read and the student understands the material. Some of the following points should be included:

- The American Revolutionary War was rooted in a belief that the American colonies had a right to economic liberty and political autonomy.

- Despite vehement opposition to the First Bank of the United States, President George Washington signed the First Bank of the United States into law on April 25, 1791, along with a 20-year charter, set to expire in 1811.

- In 1816, after the War of 1812, the Second Bank of the United States was born with a 20-year charter.

- The policies of these early central banks led to a series of booms and busts, which are a common trait of an economy with a central bank.

- In 1828, Andrew Jackson was elected president. His one guiding mission was to "kill the Second Bank."

- After a long struggle, Jackson succeeded in destroying the Second Bank of the United States.

- The period from 1837 to 1862 was known as the Free Bank Era.

- Despite numerous warnings — and two past

failures — the Federal Reserve Act was passed by the U.S. House of Representatives on December 22, 1913. The next day, just two days before Christmas, the Senate passed it and President Woodrow Wilson signed it into law.

- With the passage of the Federal Reserve Act, the greatest fears of America's founding fathers came true as our nation became enslaved to private banking interests.

Chapter Six, Worksheet 2

1) a central bank

2) debt

3) All the perplexities, confusions, and distresses in America arise, not from defects in their constitution or confederation, not from a want of honor or virtue, so much as from downright ignorance of the nature of coin, credit, and circulation.

4) taxes

5) tax

6) It sought to outlaw America's colonial scrip and replace it with money issued by the Bank of England.

7) Less than a year

8) the Tea Act

9) President Andrew Jackson

10) the cry of "taxation without representation." Followed by the American Revolutionary War

11) Alexander Hamilton

12) U.S. Secretary of State Thomas Jefferson; He believed that a central bank was clearly forbidden by the Constitution. Jefferson wrote: "I believe that banking institutions are more dangerous to our liberties than standing armies. . . . If the American people ever allow private banks to control the issue of their currency, first by inflation, then by deflation, the banks and corporations that will grow up around them will deprive the people of all property until their children wake up homeless on the continent their fathers conquered. . . . The issuing power should be taken from the banks and restored to the people, to whom it properly belongs."

13) First, they encourage borrowing by creating "cheap" money through a reduction in interest rates, which increases the overall money supply. Then, the central bank raises interest rates, leading to credit defaults, foreclosures, and bankruptcies. This allows the bankers to purchase properties, businesses, and smaller banks for "pennies on the dollar."

14) Even a casual reading of the U.S. Constitution demonstrates that Congress is only authorized to create coins with fixed "weights and measures" — not paper money.

15) While the Constitution does permit Congress to coin money, it does not give them permission to outsource this responsibility to an outside institution.

16) George Washington

17) $8 million; an average of 72 percent

18) the power of borrowing

19) the Rothschilds—Nathan Rothschild, a powerful European central banker

20) war

Chapter Six, Worksheet 3

21) the Rothschild family

22) in the wake of the war, the United States was crippled by inflation and rising unemployment

23) No

24) "boom and bust"

25) "History records that the money changers have used every form of abuse, intrigue, deceit, and violent means possible to maintain their control over governments by controlling the money and its issuance."

26) a. It concentrated the nation's financial strength in a single institution

b. It exposed the government to control by foreign interests

c. It served mainly to make the rich richer

d. It exercised too much control over members of Congress

e. It favored northeastern states over southern and western states

27) "...den of vipers and thieves. I have determined

to rout you out, and by the Eternal God, I will rout you out!"

28) "I killed the bank."

29) the Free Bank Era

30) the American Civil War

31) to fund the costs of the war

32) Instead of vesting power into just one central bank, this new act made provisions for the federal government to control a number of national banks. These national banks were then responsible for purchasing federal government bonds with their own created bank notes. The importance of this act should be noted, as it helped establish our current debt-based monetary system, which allows our federal government to create money out of thin air with the help of the Federal Reserve Banking system.

33) "The few who can understand the system will either be so interested in its profits, or so dependent on its favors, that there will be no opposition from that class, while on the other hand, the great body of the people, mentally incapable of comprehending the tremendous advantages that capital derives from the system, will bear its burdens without complaint and perhaps without even suspecting that the system is inimical to their interests."

34) "I see in the near future a crisis approaching. It unnerves me and causes me to tremble for the safety of my country . . . the Money Power of the country will endeavor to prolong its reign by working upon the prejudices of the people, until the wealth is aggregated in a few hands and the Republic is destroyed. I feel at this moment more anxiety for the safety of my country than ever before, even in the midst of war."

35) "My agency in promoting the passage of the National Banking Act was the greatest financial mistake in my life. It has built up a monopoly which affects every interest in the country."

36) The Panic of 1907

37) the Federal Reserve Act

38) mystery

39) government

40) secrecy; alarming

Chapter Six, Worksheet 4

41) "If it were to be exposed publicly that our particular group had gotten together and written a banking bill, that bill would have no chance whatever of passage by Congress."

42) control

43) "Whoever controls the money of a nation, controls that nation. . . . Whosoever controls the volume of money in any country is absolute master of all industry and commerce. . . . And when you realize that the entire system is very easily controlled, one way or another, by a few powerful men at the top, you will not have to be told how periods of inflation and depression originate."

44) crime

45) to get the controversial bill through the Senate with as little debate as possible

46) President Woodrow Wilson

47) pennies; control

48) increasing wealth and consumer excess

49) October 1929

50) Very little

51) The Executive Order 6102 authorized the confiscation of all privately owned gold held by U.S. citizens. In exchange for their gold, Americans would receive paper money. The penalties for violating this Gold Seizure Law: a $10,000 fine and/or ten years in prison.

52) the central bankers, their rich banking friends, and their prime customers

53) President Woodrow Wilson, the president who signed the Federal Reserve Act into law

54) ruled; controlled; dominated

55) International bankers make money by extending credit to governments. The greater the debt of the political state, the larger the interest returned to the lenders.

56) "Banking was conceived in iniquity and was born in sin. The bankers own the earth. Take it away from them, but leave them the power to create deposits, and with the flick of the pen they will create enough deposits to buy it back again. However, take it away from them, and all the great fortunes like mine will disappear and they ought to disappear, for this would be a happier and better world to live in. But, if you wish to remain the slaves of bankers and pay the cost of your own slavery, let them continue to create deposits."

57) with the establishment of the Federal Reserve Banking System on December 23, 1913

58) indebted

59) "we the people"

60) borrow

61) enslaved

Chapter Seven, Worksheet 1

Summary—The student's summary will vary but should show the chapter has been read and the student understands the material. Some of the following points should be included:

- Modern fiat money is debt. Each U.S. dollar represents a loan that must be paid back with interest to the Federal Reserve.

- The Federal Reserve serves as the official "lender of last resort" to the U.S. government as well as to other institutions that it considers "too big to fail."

- When the Federal Reserve issues a loan, it creates the money out of thin air.

- Fractional-reserve banking legally allows banks to maintain only a fraction of their total customer deposits at any one time.

- The FDIC was created in the wake of the Great Depression to restore confidence in the nation's banking system.

- Human labor represents the banker's profit.

Chapter Seven, Worksheet 2

1) debt

2) a. The first method of funding is through the collection of taxes, tariffs, and fees.

   b. The second way is to borrow money.

3) the U.S. Treasury Department. The Treasury Department responds to the government's request for money by printing treasury bonds, which it then sells to various buyers through public auctions.

4) the Fed is virtually required to step in and

purchase all excess treasury bonds that are not sold to the public.

5) The Federal Reserve Bank

6) it simply prints the money, thus creating it "out of thin air"

7) debt

8) several large private banks

9) Through the increased government demand for borrowed money that is generated by war.

10) to lend as much money to the government as possible

11) Public

12) Congress — not a central bank controlled by private banking interests

13) 1913

14) inflation

15) When the Fed loans currency to the government, it only creates the principal, not the interest.

16) because it was never created in the first place!

Chapter Seven, Worksheet 3

17) Federal Reserve

18) Note

19) lending

20) fractional-reserve

21) The Federal Reserve

22) raise

23) Because when a bank issues a loan, it does so under the assumption that it will be paid back in full with interest. For this simple reason, they are considered to be assets of the bank. Banks are allowed to make loans from their "assets."

24) ten

25) withdraw

26) FDIC

27) $900,000

28) bankrupt

29) The money disappears from the system.

30) money

31) Because the interest that must be paid back on every outstanding loan has never been created.

32) bankruptcies; foreclosures

33) "This is a staggering thought. Someone has to borrow every dollar we have in circulation, cash or credit. We are absolutely without a permanent money system. When one gets a complete grasp of the picture, the tragic absurdity of our hopeless position is almost incredible, but there it is."

Chapter Eight, Worksheet 1

Summary—The student's summary will vary but should show the chapter has been read and the student understands the material. Some of the following points should be included:

- In 1980, America was the world's largest creditor nation. In 2012, America has become the world's largest debtor nation in all of recorded world history.

- America has carried a national debt every year since 1791, with the exception of 1835 when President Andrew Jackson paid off national debt.

- Some of the primary causes of the increasing in our national debt include a dependence upon deficit spending, excessive military spending, entitlement spending, and a dramatic increase in the number of government employees.

- History shows that both political parties have contributed to America's growing debt crisis.

- The only true incentive for a modern U.S. politician is re-election.

- As of 2012, the Federal Reserve is the single largest owner of America's $15.5 trillion national debt.

- In 2011, the U.S. paid $454 billion in interest payments alone on the national debt.

Chapter Eight, Worksheet 2

1) "The rich rules over the poor, and the borrower is servant to the lender."

2) If you are an American citizen, this debt belongs to you . . . and to your children . . . and your grandchildren.

3) Deficit spending

4) the massive debt increase

5) "The era of big government is over."

6) By making promises to massively reduce the size of government through draconian spending cuts. Through a proposed "contract," Republicans promised to demonstrate great "fiscal restraint" and to finally bring the era of "big government" to an end.

7) increase

8) The total national debt increased by an astounding 86 percent, growing by an average of $662 billion each year he was in office.

9) Former President Obama openly continued the same destructive economic policies and disastrous foreign policy measures as his predecessors.

10) limited

11) employees

12) 14

13) deceased

14) welfare; warfare

15) They are often vilified by the corporate-controlled mainstream media and then their proposed spending cuts are used as a weapon against them by their political opponents.

16) re-elected

17) voters

18) gain

19) entitlements

20) 1. The Federal Reserve and Intergovernmental Holdings

   2. China

   3. Other Investors/Savings Bonds

   4. Japan

   5. Pension Funds

   6. Mutual Funds

   7. State and Local Governments

   8. The United Kingdom

   9. Depository Institutions

   10. Insurance Companies

21) outspend

22) "the most powerful force in the universe."

23) quadruple

24) emergency

25) responsibility

Chapter Nine, Worksheet 1

Summary—The student's summary will vary but should show the chapter has been read and the student understands the material. Some of the following points should be included:

- The U.S. Congress passed the Social Security Act in 1935 as a part of the New Deal.

- A baby boomer is defined as an American born between 1946 and 1964.

- There are approximately 78 million baby boomers in America.

- Over 10,000 Americans will reach the age of 65 every single day from 2011 to 2030.

- The unfunded entitlement liabilities for these 78 million Americans total $118 trillion.

- In 1935, an estimated 42 workers paid into Social Security for every retiree. By 1950, this ratio had decreased to 16.5 workers for every retiree. In 2012, only 1.75 workers are paying into the system for each one of the 43 million retirees currently drawing a Social Security check.

- U.S. lawmakers have not created a plan to save America's entitlement programs from insolvency. It is projected that the Social Security system will become insolvent in 2036. Medicare will become insolvent even earlier, in 2024.

- Failing government benefits, faltering pensions, longer life expectancies, and dismally low savings rates make this a noxious recipe for disaster.

- My personal financial strategy for weathering the retirement crisis is through the creation of multiple streams of income.

Chapter Nine, Worksheet 2

1) As the nation's first baby boomer, born one second after midnight on January 1, 1946, she was the first to file for U.S. Social Security benefits. The first of over 78 million baby boomers, to be more exact.

2) primary

3) dependents

4) twice

5) "the single greatest economic challenge of our era"

6) moral

7) unfunded

8) 2036

9) insolvent

10) viable

11) funded; trusted

12) chaos

13) retirement

14) by delaying their retirement plans, or just giving up on retirement all together.

Chapter Ten, Worksheet 1

Summary—The student's summary will vary but should show the chapter has been read and the student understands the material. Some of the following points should be included:

- The artificial demand and perceived safety of the U.S. dollar and debt securities, created by the petrodollar system, are the primary reasons for the dollar's continued global status.

- I forecast that by the end of this decade, a currency other than the dollar will replace the U.S. dollar as global reserve currency.

- The fall of the petrodollar system is the key leading indicator of the coming collapse of the U.S. dollar.

- The three possible solutions to our nation's debt crisis are to raise taxes, cut spending, or borrow money. It is not feasible for an individual or the government to spend its way out of debt.

- One of the responsibilities of the Federal Reserve is to act as the federal government's "lender of last resort," buying U.S. debt securities when there are no investors left.

- Many foreign nations, including China, Russia, and India have recently reduced their holdings of U.S. debt securities, indicating that foreign nations are keenly aware of our nation's financial woes.

- When the desire to hold U.S. debt securities declines, and when no one needs U.S. dollars to purchase oil, massive inflation will soon follow.

Chapter Ten, Worksheet 2

1) purchasing

2) accountability

3) trend

4) gold; oil

5) a. the artificial demand created by the petrodollar system

   b. the global demand for the perceived safety of U.S. debt securities

   c. no current competitor to the dollar

6) India, Iran, China, Russia

7) Gold and foreign government bonds

8) rival

9) replacement

10) currency

11) export

12) Foreign nations who had formerly found it beneficial to hold U.S. dollars would suddenly find that they no longer needed the massive amounts that they were holding. This massive amount of dollars, which would no longer be useful to foreign nations, would come rushing back to their place of origin . . . America. Obviously, an influx of dollars into the American economy would lead to massive inflationary pressures within our economic system.

13) provoke

14) 40

15) Washington

16) discipline; realism; fortitude; falter

17) inadequate planning, military overextension, unrealistic political promises, dreadful demographics, poor leadership, and skyrocketing medical costs

18) deceived

19) denial

20) a. Cheap gasoline prices and government policies that protect the environment

   b. Free healthcare and low taxes

   c. Low interest rates and even lower inflation

   d. Low unemployment and less government regulation

21) spending

22) entitlements

23) financed
24) pain
25) the Federal Reserve
26) China
27) alternatives

Chapter Eleven, Worksheet 1

Summary—The student's summary will vary but should show the chapter has been read and the student understands the material. Some of the following points should be included:

- Many forms of slavery exist, including slavery to culture, entertainment, money, and debt.

- No American citizen can claim to be completely debt-free, as America's national debt belongs to its citizens.

- At the foundation of America's economic problems lies a flawed assumption that our present level of consumption and economic growth must always be the absolute minimum.

- In my opinion, America's worship of money and overconsumption will be what future observers notice most when examining our nation's ruins.

- The federal government encourages consumption (even overconsumption) and discourages personal savings via the U.S. Tax Code.

- Inflation is a stealth tax, and the fact that it is hidden makes it even more difficult to overcome.

Chapter Eleven, Worksheet 2

1) enslaved
2) happiness
3) illusion
4) There are two ways to conquer and enslave a nation. One is by the sword. The other is by debt. (President John Adams)
5) inflation
6) end
7) Overconsumption
8) churches

9) therapy
10) saving
11) Gone
12) borrowing; consumption
13) losers
14) interest
15) principal
16) inflation, bankruptcies, and foreclosures
17) Inflation
18) "Inflation is one form of taxation that can be imposed without legislation."
19) a. Interest
    b. Taxes
    c. Inflation
20) planning

Chapter Twelve, Worksheet 1

Summary—The student's summary will vary but should show the chapter has been read and the student understands the material. Some of the following points should be included:

- There are three forces working against your future wealth: corporations, media/advertisers, and financial institutions.

- Corporations are in business to find a need in the marketplace and then fill it with an appropriate product or service.

- The media is in business to promote the products and services created by corporations.

- Financial institutions are in business to loan money on products and services created by corporations that have been promoted by the media.

- When consumption becomes involuntary, as it has in our modern era, the result can lead to financial devastation.

- At no time in world history have humans lived in an era in which they are so completely dependent upon others for their basic necessities.

- Those who specialize in producing something in our economy succeed at the expense of those who specialize in consumption.

- If you are stuck on life's treadmill, the quickest way off is to re-evaluate your "needs" and your "wants."

- The easiest way to re-program your mind to think like a producer is to actually become one.

- To begin creating multiple streams of income, ask yourself this question: "What good or service can I produce that others would be willing to consume?"

Chapter Twelve, Worksheet 2

1) a. Corporations

   b. Media/advertisers

   c. Financial institutions

2) involuntary

3) corporations

4) media; advertising

5) Financial

6) every

7) producers

8) easier

9) unparalleled

10) wants; needs

11) entitlement; enterprise

12) owes

13) producing

14) multiple

15) enslave; freedom

Money Wise 🔑 Quiz Answer Keys

Quiz 1— Sessions 1–6
1) property rights
2) freedom
3) incentive
4) greed
5) socialist
6) producing
7) consuming
8) slavery
9) inheritance
10) spending
11) production
12) money
13) commodity
14) promise
15) devalued
16) standard
17) prosperity
18) slave
19) consumes
20) third party
21) guillotine
22) bitter
23) *Godonomics*
24) poor/needy
25) producer

Quiz 2 — Sessions 7–14
1) God's
2) God
3) eat
4) dualism
5) competence
6) pay
7) profit
8) enslaved
9) heart
10) paycheck
11) enemies
12) forgive
13) curiosity
14) animosity
15) gives
16) isolate
17) insulate
18) rule
19) law
20) energy
21) time
22) grime
23) moments
24) will
25) diligently

Bankruptcy of Our Nation 🔑 Quiz Answer Keys

Quiz 1 — Chapters 1–6
1) debtor
2) decrease
3) Money is . . . a medium of exchange; Money is . . . a store of value; Money is . . . a unit of account
4) Lending money not currently on deposit
5) When an increase in a nation's money supply, or inflation, becomes uncontrollable, it is called hyperinflation. Hyperinflation is one of the most dangerous economic problems that can confront a nation as it causes dramatic price increases which eventually cripple the underlying economy.
6) nothing

7) a. The World Bank

   b. The International Monetary Fund (IMF)

   c. The World Trade Organization (originally called the General Agreement on Trades and Tariffs, or GATT)

8) The U.S. dollar is issued and loaned to the United States government by the Federal Reserve Bank.

9) 1971, Richard Nixon

10) A petrodollar is a U.S. dollar that is received by an oil producer in exchange for selling oil and that is then deposited into Western banks.

11) a. It increases global demand for U.S. dollars

    b. It increases global demand for U.S. debt securities.

    c. It gives the United States the ability to buy oil with a currency it can print at will.

12) There will be a massive reduction in asset value.

13) The U.S.-led invasion was inspired predominantly by Iraq's public defiance of the petrodollar system.

14) a central bank

15) All the perplexities, confusions, and distresses in America arise, not from defects in the Constitution or confederation, not from a want of honor or virtue, so much as from downright ignorance of the nature of coin, credit, and circulation.

16) President Andrew Jackson

17) Even a casual reading of the U.S. Constitution demonstrates that the Congress is only authorized to create coins with fixed "weights and measures" — not paper money.

18) war

19) "I killed the bank."

20) mystery

21) To get the controversial bill through the Senate with as little debate as possible

22) President Woodrow Wilson

23) pennies; control

24) the central bankers, their rich banking friends, and their prime customers

25) with the establishment of the Federal Reserve Banking System on December 23, 1913

26) enslaved

27) The U.S. dollar would be linked to gold at a pre-determined fixed rate of $35 per ounce. In turn, all other currencies were then pegged to the dollar, as it was viewed as being as "good as gold." This immediate convertibility from U.S. dollars into a fixed amount of gold brought much-needed economic relief and helped to restore confidence in the global financial markets.

28) First, they encourage borrowing by creating "cheap" money through a reduction in interest rates, which increases the overall money supply. Then the central bank raises interest rates, leading to credit defaults, foreclosures, and bankruptcies. This allows the bankers to purchase properties, businesses, and smaller banks for "pennies on the dollar."

29) Under the goldsmith banking system, which became popular in 17th-century England, a person would simply deposit his gold with his local goldsmith. Much like modern banking, the goldsmith would provide the depositor with a paper receipt stating the amount of gold on deposit. If the person wanted to redeem his gold, he simply returned his paper receipt to the goldsmith. (In exchange for this convenience of keeping the gold in a safe place, the town's goldsmith would charge a small monthly maintenance fee.)

30) When a nation detaches its paper currency system from any and all commodity backing, its currency is then considered by economists to be a fiat currency. When a currency is issued by fiat, it is backed only by government guarantees, not a commodity. Fiat money has no intrinsic value. Its value is derived strictly by government law, and unlike the first two types of money (commodity and receipt) there is no natural limit to the quantity of fiat money that can be produced.

Quiz 2 — Chapters 7–12

1) debt

2) The U.S. Treasury Department. The Treasury Department responds to the government's request for money by printing treasury bonds, which it then sells to various buyers through public auctions.

3) When the Fed loans currency to the government, it only creates the principal, not the interest.

4) Because the interest that must be paid back on every outstanding loan has never been created.

5) If you are an American citizen, this debt belongs to you . . . and to your children . . . and your grandchildren.

6) limited

7) welfare; warfare

8) "the most powerful force in the universe."

9) "the single greatest economic challenge of our era"

10) 2036

11) funded; trusted

12) by delaying their retirement plans, or just giving up on retirement all together.

13) purchasing

14) gold and foreign government bonds

15) inadequate planning, military overextension, unrealistic political promises, dreadful demographics, poor leadership, and skyrocketing medical costs

16) a. cheap gasoline prices and government policies that protect the environment

    b. free healthcare and low taxes

    c. low interest rates and even lower inflation

    d. low unemployment and less government regulation

17) overconsumption

18) therapy

19) saving

20) Inflation

21) any two: corporations, media/advertisers, financial institutions

22) producers

23) unparalleled

24) wants; needs

25) entitlement; enterprise

Money Wise ➤ Test Answer Key

1) property rights	11) God's
2) freedom	12) dualism
3) incentive	13) competence
4) socialist	14) enslaved
5) producing	15) enemies
6) consuming	16) forgive
7) slavery	17) curiosity
8) spending	18) animosity
9) production	19) isolate
10) standard	20) insulate

Bankruptcy of Our Nation ➤ Test Answer Key

1) Money is . . . a medium of exchange; money is . . . a store of value; money is . . . a unit of account

2) lending money not currently on deposit

3) When an increase in a nation's money supply, or inflation, becomes uncontrollable, it is called hyperinflation. Hyperinflation is one of the most dangerous economic problems that can confront a nation as it causes dramatic price increases which eventually cripple the underlying economy.

4) the World Bank; the International Monetary Fund (IMF); the World Trade Organization (originally called the General Agreement on Trades and Tariffs, or GATT)

5) A petrodollar is a U.S. dollar that is received by an oil producer in exchange for selling oil and that is then deposited into Western banks.

6) with the establishment of the Federal Reserve Banking System on December 23, 1913

7) The U.S. dollar would be linked to gold at a pre-determined fixed rate of $35 per ounce. In turn, all other currencies were then pegged to the dollar, as it was viewed as being as "good as gold." This immediate convertibility from U.S. dollars into a fixed amount of gold brought much-needed economic relief and helped to restore confidence in the global financial markets.

8) First, they encourage borrowing by creating "cheap" money through a reduction in interest rates, which increases the overall money supply. Then the central bank raises interest rates, leading to credit defaults, foreclosures, and bankruptcies. This allows the bankers to purchase properties, businesses, and smaller banks for "pennies on the dollar."

9) Under the goldsmith banking system, which became popular in 17th-century England, a person would simply deposit his gold with his local goldsmith. Much like modern banking, the goldsmith would provide the depositor with a paper receipt stating the amount of gold on deposit. If the person wanted to redeem his gold, he simply returned his paper receipt to the goldsmith. (In exchange for this convenience of keeping the gold in a safe place, the town's goldsmith would charge a small monthly maintenance fee.)

10) When a nation detaches its paper currency system from any and all commodity backing, its currency is then considered by economists to be a fiat currency. When a currency is issued by fiat, it is backed only by government guarantees, not a commodity. Fiat money has no intrinsic value. Its value is derived strictly by government law, and, unlike the first two types of money (commodity and receipt), there is no natural

limit to the quantity of fiat money that can be produced.

11) debt

12) because the interest that must be paid back on every outstanding loan has never been created.

13) If you are an American citizen, this debt belongs to you . . . and to your children . . . and your grandchildren.

14) welfare; warfare

15) "the single greatest economic challenge of our era"

16) funded; trusted

17) inadequate planning, military overextension, unrealistic political promises, dreadful demographics, poor leadership, and skyrocketing medical costs

18) saving

19) any two: corporations, media/advertisers, financial institutions

20) needs

Economics Final ━● Test Answer Key

1) property rights

2) freedom

3) incentive

4) socialist

5) slavery

6) spending

7) production

8) competence

9) enslaved

10) curiosity

11) lending money not currently on deposit

12) A petrodollar is a U.S. dollar that is received by an oil producer in exchange for selling oil and that is then deposited into Western banks.

13) with the establishment of the Federal Reserve Banking System on December 23, 1913

14) First, they encourage borrowing by creating "cheap" money through a reduction in interest rates, which increases the overall money supply. Then the central bank raises interest rates, leading to credit defaults, foreclosures, and bankruptcies. This allows the bankers to purchase properties, businesses, and smaller banks for "pennies on the dollar."

15) Under the goldsmith banking system, which became popular in 17th-century England, a person would simply deposit his gold with his local goldsmith. Much like modern banking, the goldsmith would provide the depositor with a paper receipt stating the amount of gold on deposit. If the person wanted to redeem his gold, he simply returned his paper receipt to the goldsmith. (In exchange for this convenience of keeping the gold in a safe place, the town's goldsmith would charge a small monthly maintenance fee.)

16) When a nation detaches its paper currency system from any and all commodity backing, its currency is then considered by economists to be a fiat currency. When a currency is issued by fiat, it is backed only by government guarantees, not a commodity. Fiat money has no intrinsic value. Its value is derived strictly by government law, and unlike the first two types of money (commodity and receipt) there is no natural limit to the quantity of fiat money that can be produced.

17) debt

18) inadequate planning, military overextension, unrealistic political promises, dreadful demographics, poor leadership, and skyrocketing medical costs

19) saving

20) wants

JACOBS' GEOMETRY

A Respected Standard for Teaching Geometry

Harold Jacobs' *Geometry* has been an authoritative standard for years, with nearly one million students having learned geometry principles through the text. Now revised with a daily schedule, the text is adaptable for either classroom or homeschool use. With the use of innovative discussions, cartoons, anecdotes, and vivid exercises, students will not only learn but will also find their interest growing with each lesson. The full-color student book focuses on guided discovery to help students develop geometric awareness. Geometry is all around us. Prepare to understand its dynamic influence so much better!

Jacobs' Geometry	978-1-68344-020-8
Solutions Manual	978-1-68344-021-5
Teacher Guide	978-1-68344-022-2
3-BOOK SET	**978-1-68344-036-9**
Geometry DVD	713438-10236-8
3-BOOK / 1-DVD SET	**978-1-68344-037-6**